Training, what & how:
A comprehensive guide for new trainers

By: Moustafa El-hadidi

Self-published
2015

Copyright © 2015 by Moustafa Kamal El-hadidi

All rights reserved. This book or any portion thereof may not be reproduced or used in any manner whatsoever without the express written permission of the publisher except for the use of brief quotations in a book review or scholarly journal.

First Printing: 2015

ISBN 13 : 9781517136383

ISBN 10: 1517136385

Self-published
Maadi,Cairo

Dedication

This book is dedicated to my daughter Jumana who is 4 years at the time this book is publised, May one day she realises that I have been away from her not by choice.

Contents

Preface 9

Chapter 1: Training and the organizational environment 11
    The learning organization 11
    Training, education and experience 14
    Training needs 18
    Benefits of training 21
    Training and corporate strategy 24
    Training and systems thinking 28

Chapter 2: Training Objectives 31
    Structure of objectives 32
    Sources of information for objectives 33
    Writing performance statements 35
    Establishing standards and developing end- of-training criteria measures 37
    Dealing with attitudes 38
    Identifying the conditions 40
    The value of training objectives 42

Chapter 3: The Role of the Trainer 43
    Who are the trainers? 43
    Competencies of trainers and coaches 46
    Changing roles of the trainer 54
    The consultancy role of the trainer 57
    Marketing the training function 62
    Ethics and the trainer 67

Chapter 4: Learning Principles and Conditions 70
    Sequencing the training material 70
    Readiness of the learner 70
    Ways of learning 74
    General conditions of learning 75
    Principles and specific conditions supporting learning 78

Chapter 5: What Is a Competency 87
   How Competencies Are Built from Knowledge and Skill
   87
   How Competencies Are Measured 89
   Suggested Uses for Competency Checklists 90
   Steps to Set Up a Competency Measurement Process . 90

Chapter 6: Trainer or Instructor Competencies 92
   Competencies Required of Trainers or Instructors 92
   Competency Checklists for the Trainer or Instructor . 92
   How to Use the Competency Checklists 93

Chapter 7: Training Styles 98
   Trainer Characteristics 98

Chapter 8: Understanding Adult Learner 113

Chapter 9: Analyses for Training 121
   Job analysis 126
   Job synthesis and future-oriented job analysis 127
   Functional analysis 132
   Knowledge and topic analysis 147
   Manual skills analysis 151
   Social skills analysis 152
   Evaluating criteria 153

Chapter 10: Delivering Training 156
   Before the event 156
   On the morning of the event 158
   The delivery 159
   Your style 160
   Ending the event 162
   Organizing venues 163
   Handling learners' resistance or reluctance 164
   Lack of learners 167

Chapter 11: Instructional Systems Design 168
   Analyze, Design, Develop, Implement, Evaluate (ADDIE)
   170

Chapter 12: Evaluating Training Programs 175

Chapter 13: Measuring the Return on Investment 181

ROI Progress and Status 182
Why ROI? 190
The Concerns with ROI 192
Criteria for an Effective ROI Process 193
Barriers to ROI Implementation 196
Benefits of ROI 199
ROI Best Practices 200

Chapter 14: ROI Model 203
The ROI Model 205

Preface

The structure of this book is very simple; I kept in mind that this is for the new trainers who have just joined the training industry.

But note that I will not discuss in this book how to present in the actual training session (body language, voice…etc.) as I assume that you already have that skill.

This book starts with you from the bottom with fundamental information and all the way until you reach the return of investment which is a night mare for many people.

I have tried to simplify everything as much as I can, so please forgive me if something sounds complex or you had to read it more than once to understand it clearly.

Training, what & how
A comprehensive guide for new trainers

Chapter 1: Training and the organizational environment

Any organization is simply based and established on employees, they are the supporters of it, stake holders if I may say.

For an organization advance and survive in the rapped changing market its employees must be highly skilled by effectively implanting learning and development at the individual level whereby knowledge, skills and attitude are acquired through experience sharing, reflection, study or instruction.

Development referees to enhancement and growth of the skills, knowledge and attitude through conscious and unconscious learning. Ultimately, learning and development activities should help to improve and enhance an individual's competence and potential. However, before examining how training is initiated and organized, and how it contributes to an individual's learning and development, it is appropriate to consider the wider organizational considerations that encourage and support this enterprise.

The learning organization

Amongst the many developments that have been introduced to organizations, that of becoming a learning organization has taken on a high profile. It has also led to confusion about what it actually is and some skepticism as to whether it can exist at all. Pedler Boydell and Burgoyne (1991) give the view that 'It is not brought about simply by training individuals; it can only happen as a result of learning at the whole organization level' and, although it is difficult to define precisely, the description that they offer encompasses the key sentiments that a learning organization is 'an organization which facilitates the learning of its members and continually transforms itself'. Learning by the organization and by individuals within it is seen as critical to its survival and development. Furthermore, as Senge (2006) suggests, the learning organization 'is continually expanding its capacity to create its own future'.

Drawing upon these descriptions, a profile can be built up to show what a learning organization should be. Any organization that describes itself as a 'learning organization' recognizes the need for change and actively pursues it. This is reflected in its corporate vision and business objectives which are communicated to, and shared by, its members at all levels. In order to realize its business objectives – and, ultimately, its vision – the senior management team should show its commitment to the concept of the learning organization by the comprehensive resourcing of learning strategies and opportunities. These resources should include appropriate rewards for learning, materials, time, support and empowerment.

In order to implement the concept, many would need to develop a new perspective on the way in which they work, their status, their working relation- ships and their openness. In short, they would have to manage their own change within a change to the organizational culture. In this new culture individuals should be expected to take greater responsibility for their own development by identifying their own training needs and setting themselves challenging learning objectives. Everyone should be encouraged to learn regularly and rigorously from their work experiences and to seek out opportunities away from the workplace that provide new experiences. This learning should be supported by regular reviews with line managers, team leaders or mentors to monitor and give feedback on individual performances and learning, and to decide upon and plan future learning activities. To fully implement the concept of the learning organization, learning that may be relevant or of benefit to other individuals or to other departments should be shared. The use of technology makes this process easier and quicker once the mental hurdle of being prepared to share has been overcome. With regard to the organization itself learning, the knowledge and experience that individuals have about their own roles and their own departments, together with what they know about other organizations, can be drawn upon and put to good use by contributing to the corporate vision, objectives and strategies. Many examples can be found of people in operational roles who have discovered ways of improving processes and procedures that have resulted in an organization saving on money and materials, developing a faster reaction time or producing an improved product or service. To tap into this valuable source of ideas and initiative, individuals should be encouraged to challenge, without fear, the traditional way of doing things, and the organization should be open to any suggested change or innovation which can realistically be implemented. This could lead to opportunities to contribute to policy or strategy formulation. To further and to strengthen this approach, a continual open dialogue should take place between units and departments within the organization to exchange information and ideas, and to give feedback on the goods or services that they receive from one another. The success of this approach assumes that invisible barriers have been broken down and that an open rapport has been established.

From what has been discussed it can be seen that, essentially, learning organizations have to operate as open systems (in all senses of that term) in relation to their internal and external environments. Burgoyne (1999) believes that an organization cannot be converted into a learning organization in one grand project, but that the concept should be used to guide specific projects. However, for the concept to become a reality, a number of issues need to be addressed.

Training, education and experience

Training

A planned and systematic effort to modify or develop knowledge/skill/ attitude through learning experience, to achieve effective performance in an activity or range of activities. Its purpose, in the work situation, is to enable an individual to acquire abilities in order that he or she can perform adequately a given task or job and realize their potential.

Education

A process and a series of activities which aim at enabling an individual to assimilate and develop knowledge, skills, values and understanding that are not simply related to a narrow field of activity but allow a broad range of problems to be defined, analyzed and solved.

In terms of precision, training usually involves the acquisition of behaviors, facts, ideas, etc that are more easily defined in a specific job context. Training is more job-orientated than person-orientated. Education, on the other hand, is more person-orientated, is a broader process of change and its objectives are
less amenable to precise definition. In contrasting training and education Glaser (1962) points out that 'when the end products of learning can be specified in terms of particular instances of student performance, then instructional procedures can be designed to directly train or build in these behavior's'. If the skill to be learned is highly complex and the relevant performance is difficult to analyze and to specify, then the student may be educated more generally by providing a foundation of behavior on which the individual is expected to generalize or to transfer to similar or novel situations. A second distinction which Glaser makes is related to minimizing or maximizing individual differences. He suggests that, in training, the learning of specific behaviors implies a certain degree of uniformity within the

limits set by individual differences. By contrast, education is attempting to increase the variability of individual differences by facilitating learning in such a manner that each individual comes to behave in a way which is particular to him. Training and education (including development) can be distinguished also in terms of process. In its extreme form, training tends to be a more mechanistic process which emphasizes uniform and predictable responses to standard guidance and instruction reinforced by practice and repetition. On the other hand education is a more organic process bringing about less predictable changes in the individual. These distinctions are expressed in a diagrammatic form in Figure 1.1.

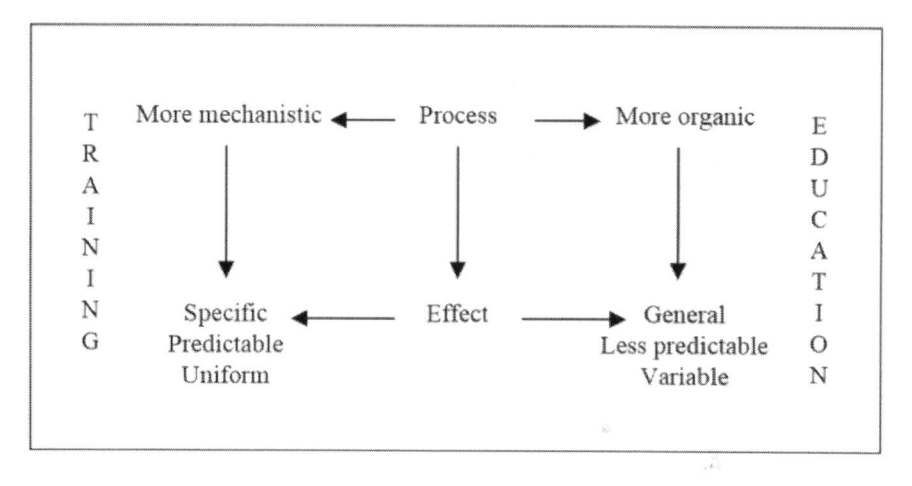

```
T       More mechanistic  ←——  Process  ——→  More organic       E
R                                                                D
A                                                                U
I                                                                C
N                ↓                 ↓                  ↓          A
I                                                                T
N         Specific        ←——  Effect   ——→  General             I
G         Predictable                        Less predictable    O
          Uniform                            Variable            N
```

Figure 1.1 The distinctions between education and training expressed in terms of process and effect

Differences between training and education also can be identified with respect to course or program content. Training aims to provide knowledge and skills and to inculcate the attitudes which are needed to perform specific tasks. Education usually provides more theoretical and conceptual frameworks designed to stimulate an individual's analytical and critical abilities.

Finally, the effects of training, education and development can be considered on a timescale. The changes brought about by training are often more immediately observable in the short term whereas education and development are more likely to show their influence in the longer term and, possibly, in a more profound way. While considerable emphasis has been placed on the way in which training and education differ, it must be appreciated that they are closely interrelated processes. The ability of an individual to acquire knowledge, skills and attitudes in a training context may depend directly or indirectly on the quality of previous educational experiences. In a similar way, education may be influenced by the skills which an individual has acquired through training and can bring to bear to exploit new learning situations. Furthermore, while concentrating on training and education, a third element which contributes to learning and development, namely planned and unplanned experience must not be minimized or overlooked. This element is a vital concomitant to formal training and education in an organizational setting. For example, management development programs often have been criticized for focusing, sometimes almost exclusively, on structured training and educational events and ignoring the value of varied and planned inter- and intra-organizational experiences.

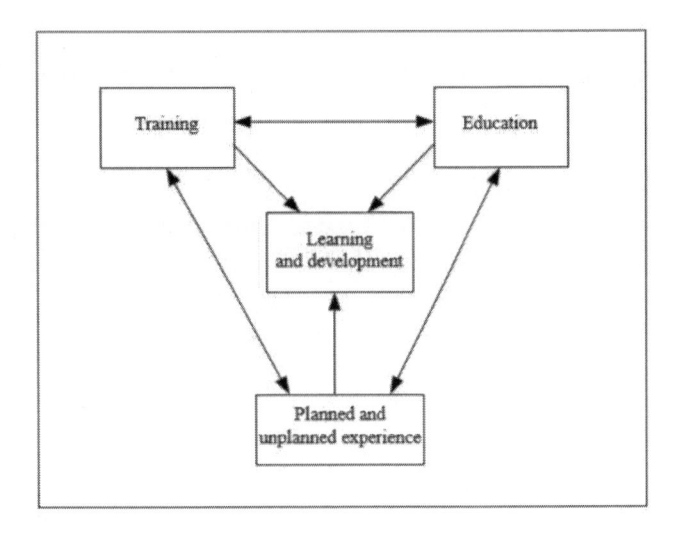

Figure 1.2 Elements that contribute to learning and development

Training, education, planned and unplanned experience are interdependent and equal partners with regard to their potential contribution to learning and development (Figure 1.2). Planned experience involves an individual carrying out a prescribed, designated task, job or role, for which they have been previously trained or educated to perform, and usually involves, at least in the early stages, some form of specialist supervision. Beyond undertaking the task, job or role on a more or less permanent basis, the potential opportunities in organizations for planned experience can take a variety of forms. These include job rotation, job shadowing, temporary attachments, visits and delegation. Too often, in the past, training and planned experience have played secondary roles to education. Each should be valued in its own right and their specific strengths in encouraging learning and development should be appreciated. Competently conducted training can expedite the acquisition of specific job- related knowledge, skills and attitudes. Education, when carried out openly and in a spirit of enquiry, can equip individuals with the intellectual perspectives and the tools of analysis that can help to guide them and their organizations through present and future exigencies. Planned experience can integrate and act as the vital catalyst and 'test bed' for the skills, techniques, ideas, etc acquired in formal training and educational settings. Unplanned learning experiences, which are inherent in the nature of many jobs or positions, can also play an important part in the acquisition and development of knowledge, skills and attitudes. If an individual has to modify or adapt what he or she had learned previously to deal with the unexpected, it can result, through a process of reflection, in a new learning experience, which enriches, extends and builds up a repertoire of appropriate responses to handle future situations. Alternatively, the inability to deal with these unanticipated contingencies may indicate a new set of learning needs that may inform future planned training, educational or experiential events.

Training needs

Turning specifically to training, because of the potentially considerable financial and psychological costs involved, a great deal of consideration has to be given to deciding whether to embark on some form of training to meet individual learning and development needs.

It is important to appreciate the circumstances which indicate whether or not training is required and there is a need to be thoroughly familiar with the methods, approaches and forms of analysis that have to be used in order to reach the decision to implement training. The criticality of this process cannot be over emphasized bearing in mind the consequences that might arise for organizations which provide too little training or no training at all when a real need exists.

Davies (1971) contributes some of the following consequences:
- Additional on-job or other forms of supplementary training.
- The slowing down of production and the underutilization of machines and equipment.
- An increase in the proportion of work rejected on inspection for not meeting the standards laid down.
- An increase in the wastage of materials and in the damage to equipment.
- Increased demands on supervisors' time.
- Job dissatisfaction because the worker is inadequately prepared to do the job. This may lead to an 'induction crisis' for new staff and to higher turnover.
- Slower or poorer service resulting in an increase in customer complaints and in a decrease in customer loyalty and interest.
- Decrease in sales and hence a reduction in profits.

The converse of the problem, that is, too much training, also has its consequences and this will be examined later. When deciding whether or not to train, the first matter of importance is to define what constitutes a training need. It is suggested that a training need can be assumed to exist when the following two conditions are met:

Condition 1	Condition 2
Training, in some form, is the most effective and the most appropriate means of addressing a learning need to overcome a current or an anticipated shortfall in performance. Or, all things being equal, training will result in current or in future performance objectives being achieved more economic- ally, thus allowing resources to be freed for alternative organizational objectives to be pursued.	Present or future job objectives are clearly linked to the organization's corporate objectives.

Training can be initiated in response to two kinds of training need; one may be described as reactive and the other proactive. The former arises out of an immediate and urgent on-job production or productivity shortfall for which a behavioral cause has been identified and separated from other possible causes. By contrast, proactive training may be closely associated with an organization's corporate strategy and manpower plan. It is very much future orientated and may come about for a number of reasons such as anticipated technical developments, the results of management development and personal replacement action and policies, etc. These two sets of needs can be contrasted also in relation to the concept of change. Boydell (1976) emphasizes that:

> Current needs are due to faults in the present situation; to solve such needs will, of course, involve change, but this change occurs after the need is identified. Future needs on the other hand, will arise as a result of change.

Apart from this present – future dichotomy another valid way of clarifying training needs is by the level at which the needs occur within the organization. A number of writers have suggested a tripartite classification:

At the organizational level
When general performance weaknesses have been observed or are anticipated in functions at or across divisional boundaries.

At job or occupational level
When distinct groups of employees have been identified as having a common need for training, eg staff within departments or functional units.

At the individual level
When performance weaknesses have been found in individual members of staff anywhere in the organization.

	Performance problem/Training need	
Level \ Time/Response	Present/Reactive	Future/Proactive
Organizational		
Job/Occupational		
Individual		

Figure 1.3 Classification of performance problems and training needs

Benefits of training

If the training needs that have been identified comply with the conditions set out above then there are numerous potential benefits to be gained by individuals and organizations from well-planned and effectively conducted training programs designed to meet those needs. Individual trainees can benefit in a number of ways. In relation to their current positions, trainees may gain greater intrinsic or extrinsic job satisfaction. Intrinsic job satisfaction may come from performing a task well and from being able to exercise a new repertoire of skills. Extrinsic job satisfaction may be derived from extra earnings accrued through improved job performance and the enhancement of career and promotion prospects both within and outside the organization to which they belong. Benefits for the organization include improved employee work performance and productivity; shorter learning time which could lead to less costly training and employees being 'on line' more quickly; decrease in wastage; fewer accidents; less absenteeism; lower labor turnover and greater customer or client satisfaction.

The above points are reinforced by Sloman (2003), in his summary of the research carried out at the University of Bath by Purcell et al (2003). These researchers have developed a People and Performance model that attempts to explain how HR practices can lead to effective performance through the influence that these practices have on discretionary behavior. The authors see discretionary behavior as '… making the sort of choices that often define a job, such as the way the job is done – the speed, care, innovation and style of job delivery.' Sloman feels that training and learning pervades the People and Performance model and is essential to the whole process. Furthermore, he believes that well-trained line managers play a crucial part in the implementation of effective human resources. He maintains that 'Ultimately they are the ones who motivate staff directly, who give them an opportunity to participate… above all they are the ones who will coach, identify skills needs, encourage development…'

Furthermore, Stewart (1996) has suggested that the training function can potentially impact in a positive and major way on the management of change. In this respect he has listed a number of key contributions that he feels the training function can make to this process. First, and most importantly, is to make sure that 'people' issues and the implications of change are raised with, and understood by, the organizational decision makers. If this does not occur then there is a serious possibility that planned change will be unsuccessful or take place too late or ineffectively to respond to environmental contingencies and demands. A second contribution consists of helping managers to develop their capacity to deal successfully with change itself. Training program and development activities can be designed to ensure that the necessary abilities to handle the uncertainties associated with change are acquired. Management development program that emphasize the managers' responsibilities for developing their own staff afford the training function the chance to make a third contribution. Linked to this is a fourth contribution, which involves the training of managers at all levels in the knowledge and skills needed to obtain the employees' commitment to change. In addition trainers can provide consultancy services to managers and staff to facilitate this process. The opportunity for training to make a fifth contribution results from the consequences of change. As these may have created a need for new knowledge, skills and attitudes within the organization, training will make its contribution through the identification of training needs and through the implementation of relevant strategies to meet these needs. Finally, the training function may make a sixth contribution by being well placed to encourage individuals, groups and the organization as a whole to examine current performance and the operating environment. Trainers are often in a good position to help diagnose the causes of poor performance and to suggest where and how improvements should be made. Stewart cites strategy workshops and team development programs as examples of training interventions that can be designed to further this critical examination. Stewart's views accord with the line taken by Frank and Margerison (1978) who emphasize that as trainers we are moving towards providing training interventions which place emphasis on solving organizational problems as well as on developing individual skills. This kind of approach has been described as Organization Development (OD). By drawing on the definitions offered by Beckhard (1969) and by French and Bell

(1999) organization development can be viewed as a long-range, planned, organization-wide effort to improve an organization's health, problem solving and renewal processes. This is done by focusing particularly on the culture of formal work teams using the theory and technology of applied behavioral science. Training can also affect an organization's culture in a more indirect way through the management of individual and group training. Cheese (1986) describes the concept and application of cascade training in marketing. This involves training a group at one level in the organization, for example, area marketing managers, and then allowing them to pass on the content and attendant attitudes to others further down the chain. From this it can be seen that cascade training is a form of communication that potentially can have an impact on individual and ultimately on group and organizational values and attitudes. More important, in some respects perhaps, than the direct and indirect effects already mentioned is the influence that the content and conduct of training can have on attitudes towards the processes of learning and development. This, in turn, can help to create a 'learning organization' that is more flexible and responsive in coping with present and future internal and external demands.

Training and corporate strategy

Hussey (1985) argues that any new corporate strategy must be looked at in the context of a number of factors or variables that affect the way in which the organization works. The relationship he sees between these organizational variables is shown in Figure 1.4.

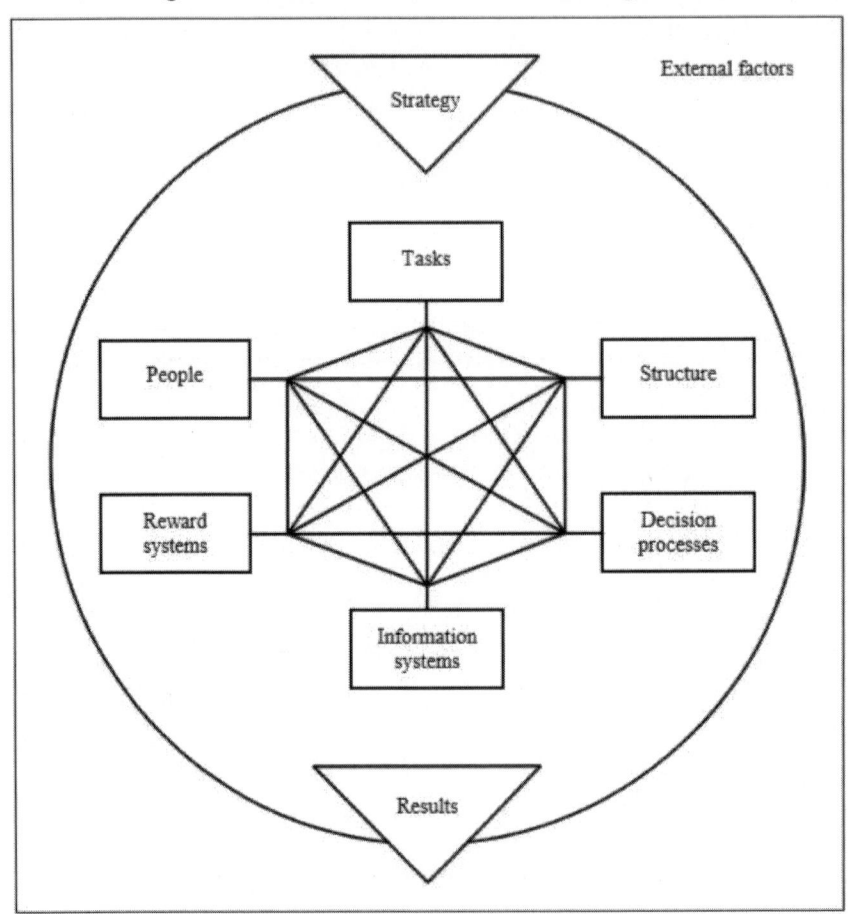

Figure 1.4 Strategy, environment and organizational variables

The clear connection which Hussey forges between strategy and the organization lead him to formulate two basic premises. First, that because an organization's activities in the education and training of management can be used to alter the organizational variables, they should be regarded as an aspect of strategy. Second, that because these activities in the education and training of management have the power to make a positive contribution to the implementation of strategy, training objectives and training initiatives should be reviewed periodically by top management and specifically when a major switch in strategy is planned.

These premises are applicable equally to broader aspects of training and indicate that training plans should be related closely to corporate strategy and built into a training policy. This policy should describe in detail the organization's commitment to training, the needs of both the business and individuals, together with opportunities for individual development. Also included should be details of budgeting, priorities, roles and processes. The assessment of training needs should be considered also from the top of the organization downwards rather than being a mainly individually orientated bottom-upwards process. Romiszowski (1981) illustrates the top downwards relationship between corporate objectives and training objectives and how this relationship can be measured by the use of an objectives matrix (Figure 1.5). The matrix shows how a single lesson objective within one particular course contributes to the achievement of objectives at higher levels. There is less likelihood of conflict or incompatibility between objectives when they are generated from the top of the organization. The Japanese experience seems to lend support to the preceding argument. On the basis of discussions with a variety of large- and medium-size Japanese companies, Brown and Read (1984) attributed their relative success in terms of productivity, by comparison with companies in the United Kingdom, partly to the fact that:

Manpower and training plans were said to be constructed in the same context and by the same process as the business plan and viewed in direct relation to it.

Much depends on how HRD is practiced in the organization. Garavan (1997) identifies five possible models which are based on the organization's perceptions of the meaning of training, development and education. In the rudimentary model a single individual takes responsibility for the HRD function but his or her activities relate mainly to operational needs, while line managers and those in professional grades look after development and education. Working to this model often results in sporadic and unstructured learning activities. The intermediate model is representative of moderate sized organizations. The HRD function is a department in its own right but the reporting line may not be to a head of HRD but to another function or indirectly to the chief executive. The range of its work is likely to include giving information about training and development activities and presenting training and developmental program. The specialized model is more sophisticated. It has a centralized HRD function and is self-sufficient to a large extent. It is staffed by full-time specialized trainers who enjoy the benefits of being well funded to offer a wide range of general and specialized activities. The developmental model puts an emphasis on continuous learning, with learning objectives being identified from real organizational problems. The model recognizes that learners direct their own learning rather than being directed by and dependent on a trainer. However, Garavan points out that there may not be a direct strategic link. Garavan's fifth model is described as the strategically linked model. This model, as its title suggests, ensures that HRD is integrated into strategic planning and that HRD practices are accepted and used by line managers as part of their everyday work. The difference that Garavan sees between this model and the others is that the previous models are focused on the maintenance of organizational stability whereas this one places an emphasis on management of change.

System level	Necessary input conditions from environment	Desired outputs	Standards (criteria)	Measuring (evaluation instruments)
Electronic industry	Continued 5 percent PA economic growth (GNP)	Increased sales of electronic equipment	Ten percent PA increase production and sales (total value)	Study of nationally published statistics
Organization X	Necessary bank approval for loans necessary recruitment for manpower	Increase in color TV production sales and after sales service	20% PA for next 3 years	Production department statistics
Training department of organization X	Necessary manpower resources new recruitment and selection policy	TV maintenance engineers	40 per annum next year rising to 60 per annum in 2 years' time Capable of repairing 20 typical faults per working day	Training department statistics on-the-job performance evaluation
Course	The necessary prerequisites in trainees Laboratory and workshop facilities	Trainees can -locate -identify -repair Faults in a color TV	Average 10 min per fault Location 100%;identification 100%; repair 80% correct	Using a special TV set programmed to simulate faults manufacture's models A, B and C
Lesson	A fault of type X in	Identify the type of	Correctly in under 1 min	Practical laboratory

	color TV model A	fault		test of fault simulator model A
Individual Lesson exercise	A live circuit and multi-test meter	Measure the voltage and resistance between any 2 points	To 5% accuracy 10 seconds per measure taken	Practical test using real test meter and a variety of standard circuits

Figure 1.5 Extract from an objectives matrix for a hypothetical training design project (Romiszowski, 1981)

Training and systems thinking

The trainer must adopt a wider, macro perspective and, as implied in Figure 1.4, accept that training is an integral part of the organization's system. But what essentially is a system? Buckley (1968) describes a system as 'a whole which functions as a whole by virtue of the interdependence of its parts'. Interdependency or interaction of its component parts is thus a prime characteristic of systems and organizations. In addition, there are a number of other features of systems which have been encapsulated in diagrammatic form by French and Bell (1999). Figure 1.6 shows that the system receives inputs from sources in the external environment. The transforming mechanism acts upon these inputs and creates outputs for users. The system may have a number of feedback mechanisms that either regulate its current output or require changes in the nature of the outputs. The organization as a whole may be described in systems terms or its component parts, eg training, recruitment, etc may be characterized in the same way.

Looking at training as a sub-system of the organization, it receives personnel, materials and information from other functional sub-systems such as marketing, from other more general sub-systems such as the one that decides and communicates corporate objectives, or from externally generated feedback. The transforming mechanism in this training sub-system produces outputs that include the knowledge, skills and attitudes acquired by trainees. The users, IE other sub-systems, should then provide the training system with appropriate feedback. This kind of model is essentially an 'open' training system which requires a proactive approach from the trainer. A 'closed' system would confine itself more to the activities contained within the circle in Figure 1.6. In the past, too much training has been of the 'closed' system variety which has made it unresponsive to organizational needs. To operate effectively in an 'open' system trainers have to be aware of, and alert to, the realities of, and the changes in, other sub-systems and organizations beyond their own which may impact on the form, content and conduct of their training efforts. For example, the launch of a new product may affect not only the knowledge content of a course in sales but also the selling skills that a sales representative needs to acquire and to exercise. In addition, the trainer must consider both the direct and planned outputs and the possible side effects of training that may influence behavior back in the place of work. A training course which has been designed in a particular way, eg using a questioning, consultative approach, may give rise to expectations in the trainees which are subsequently frustrated when they return to their work situation. Such an experience may then create negative attitudes and feelings which become part of the input to future training initiatives. This is not to suggest that constraints should be placed on particular styles of training, but rather to show that trainers should be aware of certain contextual factors which may affect the application of skills and knowledge and that these factors should be a vital input to the training system. All parts of the organization react to the inputs from other sub-systems and the external environment in their own way depending on their function. It follows that each specialized function has its own particular approach within the general framework of the organization. Training is no exception and trainers have developed their own logical or systematic approach.

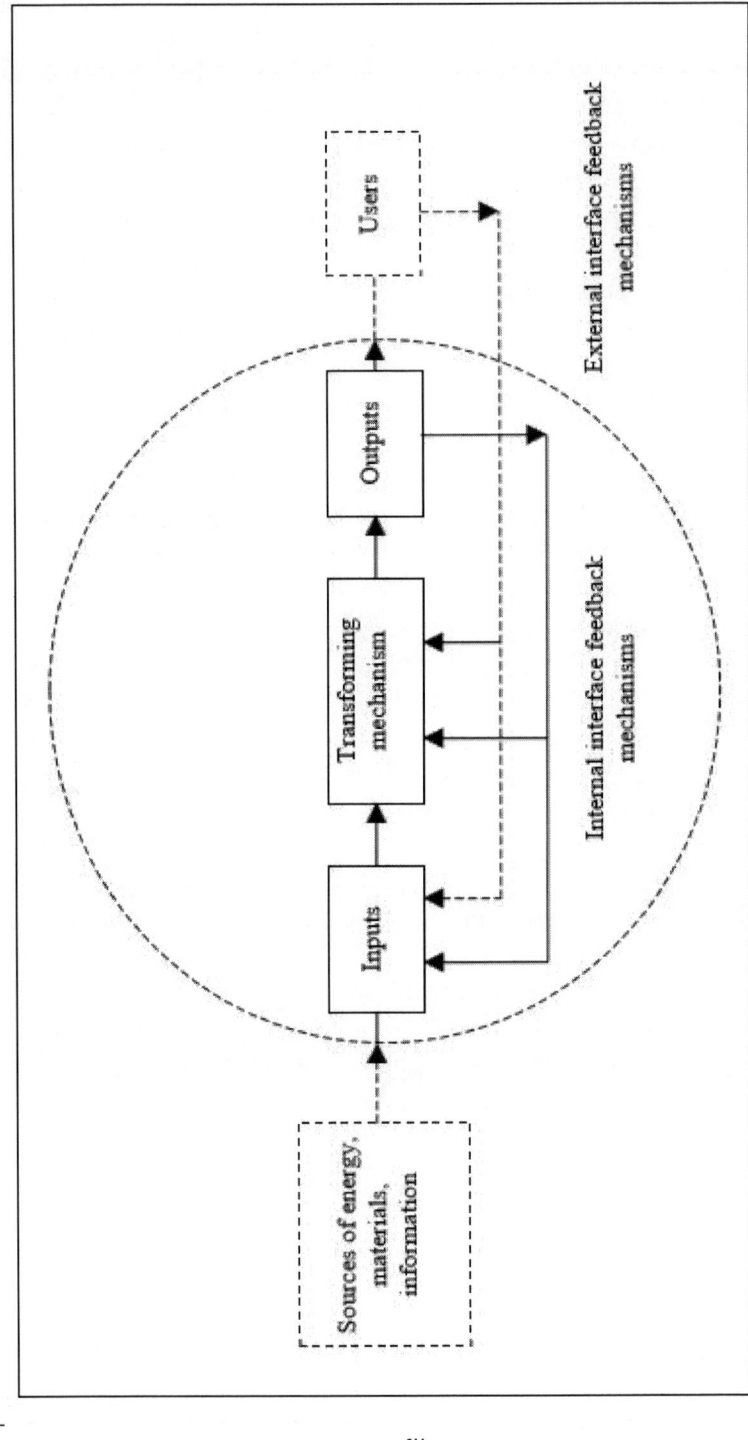

Figure 1.6 Diagram of a system in interaction with its environment (French and Bell, 1999)

Chapter 2: Training Objectives

The terms 'aim' and 'objective' are often seen as having the same meaning and are used interchangeably but in practice there is a clear and an important difference. An aim indicates or provides a general statement of intent. On the other hand, objectives spell out precisely how this is to be achieved. It can be likened to crossing a stream: the aim is to cross the stream and the objectives are the stepping stones to get there. By their nature aims are usually expressed in general terms which the following examples illustrate: 'To develop the interpersonal skills of hotel receptionists'; 'To increase line managers' knowledge and understanding of their responsibilities for health and safety'; and 'To become a competent fork lift driver'. The purpose of an objective is to state as clearly as possible what trainees are expected to be able to do at the end of their training (or at the end of stages in their training), the conditions under which they will demonstrate their learning and the standards that must be reached to confirm their level of competence and thus achieve the aim. Well-written training objectives can be used as a means to validate and evaluate training; they assist trainers to decide upon method and content of training and they provide trainees with a clear target. A comparison of the following two examples helps to illustrate the importance of having clear objectives.

1. At the end of training the trainee will be able to saw timber into different lengths.

Working to this objective it is possible that we may conjure up a picture of trainees going forth into lumber forests with chain saws, felling trees and sawing them into suitable lengths for transportation. All of this could well be ideal if the trainees were going to be employed in forestry but if the intention was to train cabinet makers, then the objective has failed in its purpose. The second example might have been more appropriate.

2. Given a tenon saw, mitre block, pencil and ruler, the trainees will be able to cut pieces from a three-metre length of 5 cm × 8 cm timber to any size stated in meters, centimeters and millimeters and to be accurate to within 2 mm.

This is a much clearer guide to what is expected although there is still room for refinement. Example 2 actually allows us to build up an accurate mental picture of the trainees at work. Before going into detail about the composition, format and presentation of objectives it will be of some benefit to distinguish between different categories of objective used in training.

Structure of objectives

The analysis of a complete objective will show that it has three main parts – the performance which trainees are expected to display at the end of their training, the conditions under which they will perform and the standards which they are expected to reach. For ease of use and for easy reference they are usually tabulated in three columns (Figure 1.7).

Performance	Conditions	Standards
Press a pair of trousers	Given: Electric steam iron Ironing board Pair of trousers	Within 10 minutes Creases to be straight and in correct position. Without damage to fabric.

Figure 1.7 Example of layout of a training objective

Another format is suggested by Romiszowski (1981). He highlights the importance of measuring the criteria or the standards of performance expected by including a column to describe the method of measurement or testing which should be used. In addition, the heading to his columns are statements rather than single words. This gives a flow to the reading of the objective which helps to give it sense (Figure 1.8).

Given the following external conditions	The student will	To the following standard	As measured by the following method

Figure 1.8 Layout of objectives (Romiszowski, 1981)

Sources of information for objectives

It can be seen from what has been discussed that a considerable amount of information about jobs, and about the tasks and skills which are contained within them, can be gathered from different forms of analysis which will have been undertaken during the previous stages. For example, the scalar diagram showing a hierarchical task analysis (Figure 1.9) could be translated into a set of objectives. A section of the scalar is reproduced below and it can be seen that the different levels of task (for servicing a petrol-driven motor car) relate directly to terminal objectives, enabling objectives and learning points.

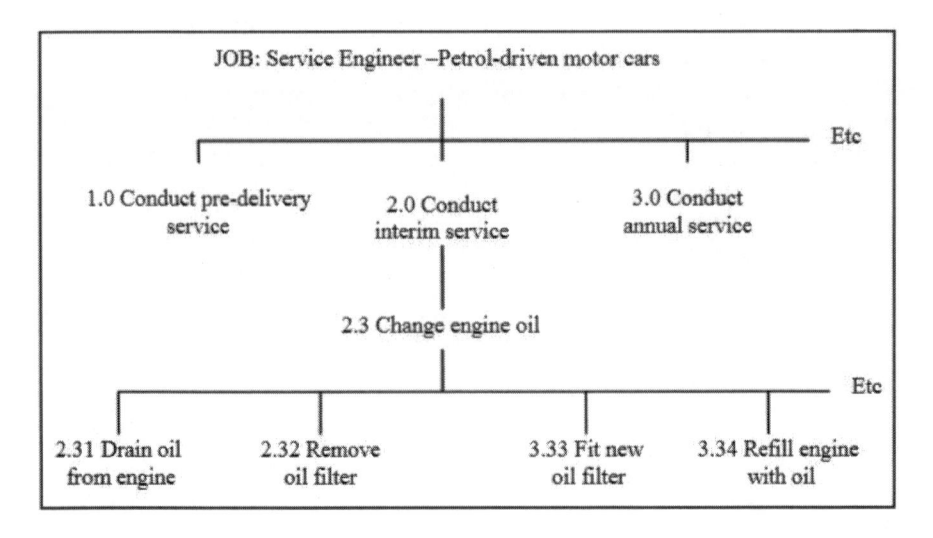

```
                    JOB: Service Engineer – Petrol-driven motor cars
                    │
        ┌───────────┼───────────────────────────┐──────── Etc
        │           │                           │
1.0 Conduct pre-delivery  2.0 Conduct         3.0 Conduct
        service           interim service     annual service
                          │
                    2.3 Change engine oil
                          │
        ┌─────────────┬───┴─────────┬─────────────┐──── Etc
        │             │             │             │
2.31 Drain oil   2.32 Remove   3.33 Fit new   3.34 Refill engine
 from engine      oil filter    oil filter       with oil
```

Figure 1.9   Extract from hierarchical task analysis

Each of the tasks is described in behavioral terms and could be used, without alteration, as the performance statements for skills-based objectives. The question would then need to be asked for each performance' 'What does the learner need to know in order to perform this task?' The answers would provide the knowledge-based objectives. In addition, the tasks and sub-tasks shown on the scalar are arranged in the sequence in which they should be undertaken and point to the order in which they should be learned. This will help with the planning of training. The analyses of tasks and skills will have categorized the knowledge, skills and attitudes which the trainee will have to acquire. The breakdown of tasks into sub-tasks and task elements will have indicated the nature of the enabling objectives and lesson objectives which are likely to emerge. Skilled workers and their supervisors will have provided an indication of the standards which are expected and close observation and interviews will have provided full details of the conditions in which the job is performed. Armed with this information the trainer should be able to write detailed and precise objectives.

Writing performance statements

The first step in writing objectives is to identify precisely what the trainee will be expected to do at the end of the training. This is written as a performance statement. Using the information obtained from the analyses of jobs and tasks, three main areas of performance will have been identified – knowledge, skills and attitudes. Behavior in these three areas can be classified in detail and a listing of appropriate performance verbs can be compiled as a reference and as a form of job aid to help the trainer to compose performance statements. This will help in the design of training and in the selection of learning strategies. The example in Figure 6.6 illustrates a basic form of such a classification. More detailed classifications or taxonomies have been developed which have analyzed behaviors into what have been described as domains. These are the taxonomies of the cognitive domain (Bloom, 1956), the affective domain (Krathwohl et al, 1964) and the psychomotor domain (Simpson, 1966). Trainers can draw upon these sources directly, when it is appropriate, or they can use them to develop classifications of their own which are appropriate to the field in which they are working. For example, when training is being investigated in a field which involves social skills, a trainer may wish to develop a closely defined set of behaviors relating perhaps to group decision making or to counseling, etc.

Knowledge	Memorization	Recall of fact and sources Recognition
Skills	Comprehension Intellectual	Understanding -Application -Analysis -Synthesis -Evaluation
	Manual	-Bodily actions and movements -Dexterity of hand and eye/hand and ear, etc -Non-verbal behavior
	Social	Oral and appropriate non-verbal behavior in one-to-one and group situations (eg interviews, meetings)
Attitudes	Accepting Valuing Being receptive	Respond willingly Show commitment Follow rules and procedures

Figure 2.0 a basic classification of knowledge, skills and attitudes

The performance statement of an objective should contain a word or a phrase that describes what the trainees are expected to do to demonstrate that they have achieved the objective.

Establishing standards and developing end- of-training criteria measures

Having written the performance statement, the next logical step is to decide how it is to be tested. However, trainers can be tempted to ignore this and either come back to it later or place the onus of responsibility for testing on the trainer. It must also be taken into account that in some instances it is not in the organizational culture or perhaps the national culture to test those who have undergone training. This is often linked with a policy of not reporting on the performance of trainees to their respective departmental heads. When this approach is employed the competence of the trainee has to be taken as an act of faith by everyone concerned and one cannot help but call this approach to question. During the investigative stages of the process a clear indication of what is expected of the fully competent job holder will have been established with the assistance of supervisors and competent workers. However, it may not be viable to train to such a standard. For example, a fully competent and experienced lathe operator may be able to produce items of high quality and in large numbers. It would be wasteful of training time to keep the trainee in training until speed had been built up. It would be more likely that the trainee would be trained to produce items to an acceptable standard in terms of quality and subsequently to develop their skills on-the-job to the standard expected of the experienced worker. In establishing the criteria, what has to be considered is the minimum acceptable level of performance before the trainee can be allowed to perform the job. This does not suggest that there should be a lowering of standards. If we are training a soldier to operate a mine detector, he would be expected to be 100% accurate before being sent ahead to clear a path for advancing troops.

The criterion measures must be a realistic test of the performance which will indicate that the trainee will be able to transfer successfully the knowledge and skills learned in training to the job situation. Many performance statements indicate very clearly what the test item should be and in some cases can be used, without alteration, as a test question. For example, the following performance statements indicate very clearly the test item:

- 'List the benefits of a personal pension policy.'
- 'Discriminate (by placing in two piles) between correctly and incorrectly completed forms.'
- 'Prune a rose bush.'

If criterion measures are not established at this stage there is the possibility that inappropriate tests may be employed. In the example given above, 'Prune a rose bush', one would expect that in the test the trainees would be given a pair of pruning shears and a rose bush which needed to be pruned so that they could demonstrate their skills. If, however, the trainees were given a question in either oral or written form which asked them to 'Describe how to prune a rose bush', there is likely to be some doubt as to whether they might actually be able to do it in practice. In deciding the criterion measures then, the trainer must consider both the appropriateness of the test and the standard which has to be reached. In many cases the standards will be easy to determine and might include numbers of test items answered correctly, measurements within certain tolerances, time factors, etc. In other cases it will be more difficult to specify and reliance will be placed upon the judgment of the trainers or instructors.

Dealing with attitudes

Objectives which are concerned with attitudes are often found to be more difficult to handle. One of the main reasons for this is that it is difficult to write such an objective within a framework headed performance, conditions and standards. More particularly it is almost impossible, in the short term, to observe and measure whether an attitude has actually changed or developed. What is observed is a behavior which suggests an attitude and many trainers argue that this is sufficient. For example, if one of the attitudinal objectives for training counter staff in a department store is 'Value all customers as essential to the survival and development of the store', it would be difficult, if not impossible, to measure whether staff did actually have such an attitude.

However, there are a number of aspects of behavior which could suggest that they do 'value all customers'. These might include helpfulness, courtesy, speedy service, smiling and the employment of other social skills. The trainer, when faced with this kind of situation, often feels that it is something of a dilemma because although staff are demonstrating behaviors which suggest an attitude, underneath they may not have any real concern about customers at all. This should not really be a dilemma; if the customers feel that they are being valued and continue to bring their custom to the store, then in many ways the objective has been achieved. Also, it is believed that when people demonstrate such a behavior over a period of time, they may find it intrinsically rewarding and, as a result, their attitudes will change to those which the organization desires. Therefore, trainers need to be more concerned with behavior rather than soul searching to confirm that attitudinal objectives have been achieved. A further problem with writing objectives for attitudes is that they do not stand alone in the same way as other objectives. Attitude, or the behavior that reflects attitude, is usually displayed within the context of other objectives. One is not courteous, helpful, caring, etc in a vacuum. These attitudinal behaviors are related to other performances such as serving a customer, advising a customer on suitability of materials, installing or repairing electrical appliances or receiving a patient. In many ways these behaviors can be seen as standards which are expected within the context of other behaviors even though the assessment of level of competence is likely to be subjective and 'to the satisfaction of the trainer/supervisor'. It has been found that often it is more appropriate to treat attitudinal objectives in this way. The following example of part of an objective indicates how this may be done.

Accounts department training

Performance	Standard
Reply to telephone enquiry from a customer relating to an account	Trainee to identify self and department in approved style. Give information requested – without error

Other aspects of attitudinal development cannot be dealt with as easily as the example given above. In the training of a trainer, for example, one of the objectives may be concerned with the preparation and planning of training sessions or lessons. While the trainee may be able to demonstrate the ability to prepare and to plan, something more may be wanted in attitudinal development, ie 'Value the need for thorough preparation and planning'. In these circumstances one cannot observe the trainee 'valuing' although the process of preparation and planning may be observed. As before, it would be expected, or at least hoped, that in time the trainee would find that preparation and planning has proved to be so important that it would come to be valued. However, while this may be long term and it may be questionable whether it should be listed as an objective, there is a clear need for those who train the trainers to be aware of such objectives. By demonstrating how much they value the need for preparation and planning themselves they can contribute significantly to the attitudes of those whom they are training. In circumstances such as these, there is every reason for listing some categories of attitudinal objectives separately so that the trainers are aware of the attitudes which they may have to display overtly in order to develop the same attitudes in their trainees.

Identifying the conditions

The various forms of analysis which were used to examine tasks and skills will have identified also the conditions in which the jobs are performed. This will provide such information as: the tools, equipment, materials and documents, etc that are used, the physical environment, assistance and supervision given as well as other general working conditions. If training is to be realistic then consideration has to be given as to how far the conditions of the job should be replicated in training. Obviously, when training is on-job or partially on-job then all or many of the conditions will be replicated. The more realistic that one makes the conditions in training then the more expensive and, possibly, the more time-consuming training becomes. Realism has to be balanced against the critical nature of the performance being trained. There would be no doubt in anyone's mind about the need for investment in complex simulators for the training of airline pilots, particularly for dealing with emergency situations. However, it can be seen that there might not always be a need for telephone networks to train some of the more basic skills in telephone techniques. Some very basic training can be done by just seating two people either side of a screen. When writing objectives the trainer has to bear in mind the conditions which exist for the job and to decide what the conditions will be for training. It follows that trainers need to be familiar with the job environment either by experience of doing the job or by familiarization visits and attachments. While replicating the working environment is one important reason for identifying and stating conditions, another reason is linked with testing. When conditions are looked at in detail, it can lead to changing the performance statement completely. The following example illustrates the point. One of the objectives for clerical officers working in an educational environment was stated as:

- 'List the subject passes in other examinations which give exemption from sections of Parts 1, 2 and 3 of the Advanced Certificate.'
- 'Advise applicants for the Advanced Certificate on exemptions awarded for subject passes in other examinations.'
- 'Given: Subject-exemption charts and specimen application forms from applicants.'

This puts quite a different perspective on training for the role of the clerical officer. Another feature of deciding the conditions for training objectives is uniformity. Not all training takes place in one location. In some large organizations the training may be delivered as courses in geographically dispersed centers or as on-job training. A clear statement of the conditions to be applied in training will ensure greater uniformity. For example, in word-processor training there would be a need to specify what kind of package should be used, the nature of subject matter for dictation or copy typing, the use of technical terms and foreign words, the length of passage, etc.

The value of training objectives

From what has been discussed so far it can be seen that there are distinct benefits to be gained from investing time in writing objectives:

- They prevent teaching too much or too little. Too much training is costly and if irrelevant material is included it can be confusing. Too little training results in further performance problems and the cost and trouble of rectifying matters.
- They provide guidelines for course design and are the basis for producing enabling objectives and learning points.
- They clarify for trainers/tutors and for trainees precisely what their goals are in training.
- They provide the basis for measuring the effectiveness of training in terms of the knowledge, skills and attitudes expected of the trainees, the minimum acceptable performance standards and the conditions under which the performance is measured.
- They provide a link between training needs and the training which is delivered so that the training can be validated.
- They provide a first point of reference for any investigation or review of training.

Chapter 3: The Role of the Trainer

In the context of training, many trainers in both the public and private sectors have found that they have had to compete directly with 'outside' providers and other providers within their own organization. When responsibility for training has been devolved and smaller units empowered to make their own arrangements there have been mixed outcomes. The sharpening of the business skills of trainers has in many cases enhanced the quality of training, but the downside has often been inadequate training delivered at low cost. This means that trainers must become more business orientated and develop their knowledge and skill to make a measurable contribution. This will involve establishing the position of training in the organization, identifying the changing roles of the trainer, deciding what kind of trainers are needed to meet these roles, marketing the training function and measuring its effectiveness in business terms.

Who are the trainers?

It has always been considered that line managers and supervisors, or their equivalents (team leaders, charge hands etc) have a responsibility for training. This aspect of their work has not always been discharged effectively. Reasons for this have included (with some justification) that they have been too busy performing other managerial tasks and that training is the responsibility of the training department. Their argument is understandable in a number of respects, especially when there are many staff who need the same kind of training. However, there are aspects of all jobs where specialist training or specific job training is needed, and only the manager or team leader can provide that training. In most instances this is carried out, but it is regarded as 'showing' someone what to do rather than training. The line manager's function also includes discussing training and development needs with individuals, arranging appropriate training and assessing its effectiveness in the workplace. Again, this is not always seen as being involved in training. In the same way, individuals are trained on a one-to-one basis by members of their peer group who do not see themselves as trainers. Those working on open-learning programs are often helped by 'supporters' who may know little about the subject matter, but who make an important contribution to learning by providing encouragement and general support. From this scenario it can be seen that there are many who could be described, to varying degrees, as 'trainers'. Whilst accepting that a variety of people have a hand in training, and that their roles cannot be ignored, it is usually those whose full-time role is training who are described as 'trainers' and who regard themselves as 'professionals'. However, it is not always clear what is meant by the term 'professional trainer'. In fact, there are at least three possible meanings which readily come to mind. It could mean the training specialist who has been brought into the organization from outside; it could mean the career specialist within the organization who has decided to make his or her future in training; or it could refer to those who, as part of their career plan, spend some time in training during which they develop considerable expertise in, and commitment to, training. There is no reason why all three categories shouldn't exist side by side and be regarded as 'professionals'. The most important factor is that training staff should be of a high caliber so that they can contribute to making the training departments the centers for excellence that they should be. The career specialists in training are vital to the training function because of its scope and the need for expertise. This book has indicated the demands which are made on trainers generally and there is scope for further specialization within training as new technology offers alternative methods of delivery which need to be researched and subsequently employed through the application of specific skills. Developing the general and the specific skills cannot be achieved by a short- term training and development program. It takes a considerable time to build up a competence and confidence level to take on the role of a training specialist. Many who have reached this level have done so just at the time when, in the normal course of events, they are moved back to their main career discipline. It is at such a point when potential is just about to be realized that the organization loses one of its most useful assets. Organizations which allow and encourage their personnel to make their careers in training will get a valuable return from their contribution. From this it might be suggested that it is a waste to take into the training department those who are only likely to stay for perhaps two years before pursuing their careers in other directions. This is not strictly true and it is believed that training departments need staff who fall into this category. It is true that the gifted amateur approach is no longer appropriate and that a thorough training is needed. The short-stay trainer is not only able to bring recent practical experience to the training department but subsequently takes a knowledge of, and hopefully a commitment to, training back to the main operational functions of the organization. The professionalism of the trainers who are in this category is reflected partly in the expertise which they develop and also in the attitude that they display towards training and their own need to be trained.

A deficit in this area is often found in the training manager who may believe that the training function can be managed with very little knowledge of training or, even worse, the manager who may believe that the little knowledge that he or she has represents the sum total of what training is all about. Training managers must be credible in the eyes of their staff and be given thorough training rather than the overview which they feel is all that they need. Apart from adopting a sensible selection policy and devising proper training, meaningful career paths, development programs and reward systems should be developed for both career and short-stay trainers. In the case of career trainers working in large training departments it may be feasible to draw up coherent promotion structures. However, if the training section is relatively small, but part of an integrated personnel department then it may be sensible on occasions to create personnel specialists rather than career trainers. These individuals would spend several periods in training as their career and promotions take them through the various specialisms within the personnel function, eg industrial relations, job evaluation, recruitment and selection, etc, thus combining the advantages of being pure career trainers with those of the short-stay trainer. It could ensure that they 'keep in touch' with training whilst at the same time broaden their perspectives by operating elsewhere. In addition their 'pick-up' on re-entering the training sphere should be relatively smooth. It is essential that the true short-stay trainer, going back to his or her main operational area after a spell in training, does not perceive this period as a sentence in the organizational 'gulag'. The secondment must be linked clearly to the individual's past and future experiences and must be seen to contribute to the development of knowledge and skills of value to their careers. Above all, the period in training must not adversely affect an individual's promotion prospects by apparently taking them out of their mainstream activity and forcing them to mark time.

Competencies of trainers and coaches

When the strategies and tactics for training programs are selected, the skills demanded of the trainers are often overlooked. The assumptions are made that those who are full-time trainers are Omni competent and that those who could be described as occasional trainers need only to have technical competence to be able to train or coach others. Trainers who are involved in the delivery of training are likely to have to call upon a variety of skills which is not always appreciated by some managers or by the individuals themselves. There is a range of specific skills that is needed to undertake one-to-one training, coaching, training groups, facilitating, counseling to support distance learning, and to write distance learning materials. However appropriate the strategy or tactic may be when measured against the constraints, target population, budget and the principles of learning, unless the trainers have been selected and trained to meet high standards, the intended learning outcomes will not be met. In order to decide what criteria should be used for their selection and also what their training needs are, it is important to identify the positive and negative qualities found in trainers. The characteristics which have been observed in poor trainers include:

- Adopting a highly directive style of teaching which does not allow participation or confirmation that learning has taken place;
- Making unrealistic assumptions about the trainees' level of knowledge or failing to establish their level of knowledge in the first place;
- Displaying impatience or intolerance when trainees fail to understand or are slow to learn;
- Lacking commitment to the subject being taught or to training as an important function in the organization;
- lacking in verbal/oral skills;
- trying to teach too much too quickly;

- refusing to accept criticism or advice on teaching methods;
- having an untidy appearance;
- creating dependency by either imposing solutions on the learner or being too quick to suggest ideas or ways forward;
- trying to be too clever and win or score a point against the learner;

It might be that sophisticated selection and assessment instruments need to be developed in order to find the best trainers or coaches. The training centers of some organizations have potential tutor courses which provide the opportunity for candidates to observe current training in progress, to talk with tutors and to present a period of instruction or run one-to-one sessions so that their potential can be judged. When this is not possible or when it is not cost-effective to employ a selection strategy, which might be the case with one-to-one trainers, a simple matching system can be used which compares the qualities of the potential trainer with those of a good trainer or coach.

Above all, the people selected should actually want to be trainers or coaches. In the past it has been thought that the subject 'expert' should be ideal for such roles. Undoubtedly, in most circumstances there is a requirement for subject competence. However, it may be more profitable in the long term to improve the technical competence of someone with potentially good trainer qualities rather than try to develop the interpersonal skills, etc of the subject 'expert' who is unsuited or unwilling.

In order to structure a training session the trainer needs to have diagnostic skills and a range of technical, interpersonal and judgmental skills. The technical skills would include preparing and planning a period of instruction, deciding the style and methods of presentation, organizing the logistics of syndicate, role-playing and other activities, making training aids and using them correctly.

There is a need to develop questioning skills, to design tests or test sample pieces. These are closely associated with the judgmental skills required to make an appraisal and gain an impression of the nature of the trainee, to set realistic goals during training and to recognize when the trainee is sufficiently competent to apply what has been learned.

The interpersonal skills which the one-to-one trainer and coach have to apply are described by Megginson and Boydell (1979) as being similar to those required by the skillful counselor. This includes attending, observing, remaining silent, drawing out, giving and receiving feedback and suspending judgment. The importance of these skills become clear when it is remembered that coaching is undertaken at all levels in the organization where individuals are being developed to undertake greater responsibilities. The same, and additional skills, have to be exercised by the trainer who is involved with groups of learners. This is illustrated by Anderson who, in describing the CTAT course model, suggests that each of the stages require the use of a range of training methods and the application of a complex mix of skills that tutors would need to possess and exercise if all four stages of the process are to be realized successfully. Figure 12.1 illustrates the breadth of this range of methods and skills.

Without a thorough appreciation of, and training in, the appropriate skills, then activities such as syndicate exercises, discussions, role-plays, etc can deteriorate into time fillers or rest periods for the trainer. These activities or tactics should be used to achieve objectives and demand a range of skills from the trainer which, in addition to those listed above, include listening, analyzing, correcting, guiding, prompting, controlling and summarizing. In exercising these skills the trainer acts as a facilitator which is quite different from the role which many trainers usually adopt. One of the reasons that tactics such as role-play and discussion may not be effective is because the trainer, or those who have designed the training, do not understand the demands that facilitating makes on the trainer.

In discussing one-to-one and group training, it has been seen that control over the direction and content of the training has been exercised by the trainer. Facilitating places the trainer in a position where he or she becomes an enabler for students to learn by themselves. The trainer and the trainees become interdependent and draw upon one another's knowledge and skills to achieve the learning objective. In effect, control over the learning process passes in varying degrees, depending on the tactic, to the trainee. Figure 2.1 illustrates the difference in tutor roles.

LEARNING METHODS
concrete experience

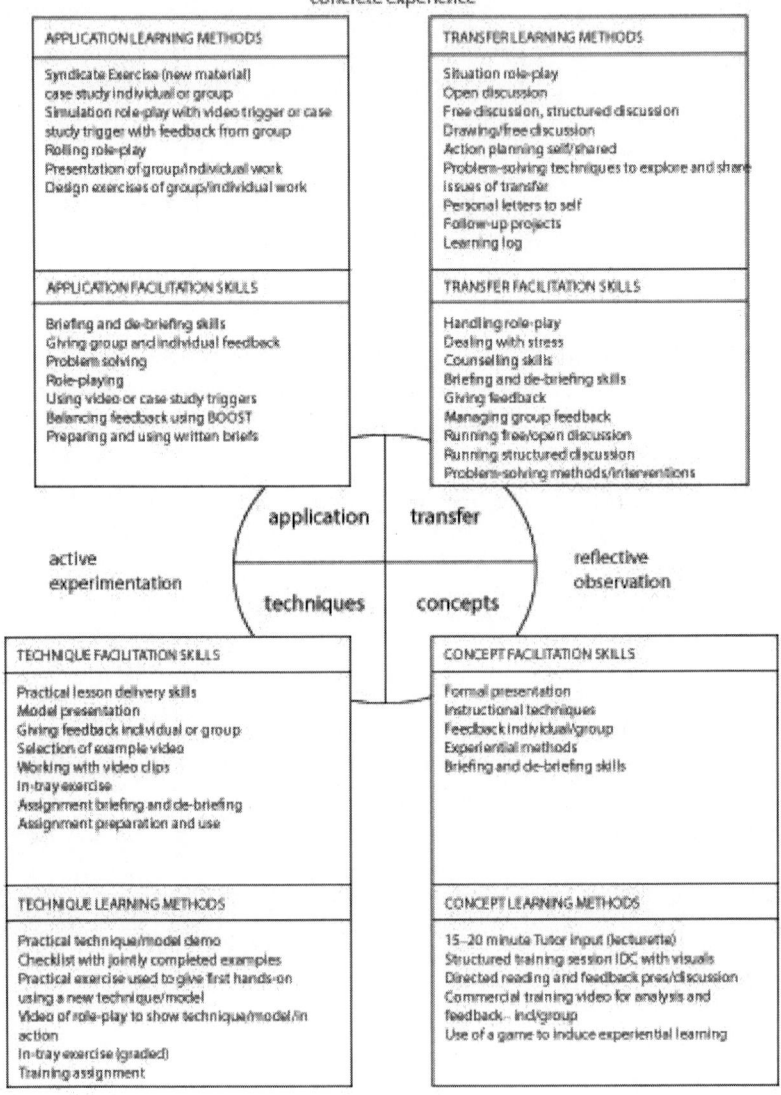

APPLICATION LEARNING METHODS
- Syndicate Exercise (new material)
- Case study individual or group
- Simulation role-play with video trigger or case study trigger with feedback from group
- Rolling role-play
- Presentation of group/individual work
- Design exercises of group/individual work

APPLICATION FACILITATION SKILLS
- Briefing and de-briefing skills
- Giving group and individual feedback
- Problem solving
- Role-playing
- Using video or case study triggers
- Balancing feedback using BOOST
- Preparing and using written briefs

TRANSFER LEARNING METHODS
- Situation role-play
- Open discussion
- Free discussion, structured discussion
- Drawing/free discussion
- Action planning self/shared
- Problem-solving techniques to explore and share issues of transfer
- Personal letters to self
- Follow-up projects
- Learning log

TRANSFER FACILITATION SKILLS
- Handling role-play
- Dealing with stress
- Counselling skills
- Briefing and de-briefing skills
- Giving feedback
- Managing group feedback
- Running free/open discussion
- Running structured discussion
- Problems-solving methods/interventions

application | transfer

active experimentation | reflective observation

techniques | concepts

TECHNIQUE FACILITATION SKILLS
- Practical lesson delivery skills
- Model presentation
- Giving feedback individual or group
- Selection of example video
- Working with video clips
- In-tray exercise
- Assignment briefing and de-briefing
- Assignment preparation and use

TECHNIQUE LEARNING METHODS
- Practical technique/model demo
- Checklist with jointly completed examples
- Practical exercise used to give first hands-on using a new technique/model
- Video of role-play to show technique/model in action
- In-tray exercise (graded)
- Training assignment

CONCEPT FACILITATION SKILLS
- Formal presentation
- Instructional techniques
- Feedback individual/group
- Experiential methods
- Briefing and de-briefing skills

CONCEPT LEARNING METHODS
- 15–20 minute Tutor input (lecturette)
- Structured training session IDC with visuals
- Directed reading and feedback pres/discussion
- Commercial training video for analysis and feedback – ind/group
- Use of a game to induce experiential learning

abstract conceptualization

Figure 2.1 The CTAT model and facilitation and learning methods

In the facilitating mode the trainees contribute knowledge, skills and experience which have been acquired over a number of years which they can share with others. Also they are likely to bring with them their own learning style, self- confidence, esteem, motives for learning, prejudices and expectations. Facilitators have to adapt their approach to meet the needs of the trainees and individuals within the group which could involve a change in, or development of, the trainer's attitudes. There must be an acceptance of openness within the group so that it can establish its own ground rules to work together as a cohesive unit and that the facilitator is a resource for the group to draw upon to direct activity and contribute to their learning. In performing this function, the facilitator will need to exercise a variety of skills. There is a need to be aware of, and to monitor, the individual learning and emotional needs of members of the group, to create a secure climate to structure the learning experiences and activities of the group and to control the learning experiences so that they remain relevant and that the objectives are achieved. The role of facilitator is demanding and not all trainers may be able to adapt to it. Training departments that plan to use their trainers as facilitators could overcome potential problems by being more rigorous in the assessment of attitudes and skills of potential trainers. Rogers (1969) identifies a range of qualities of facilitative trainers which can be used to build a profile for selection:

- less protective of their own constructs and beliefs than other trainers;
- more able to listen to students, especially to their feelings;
- able to accept the ideas of students even if they are seen to be troublesome, provoking, etc;
- able to devote as much time to developing relationships with individuals and the group as to training content;
- able to accept positive and negative feedback and use it in their own development

Clarke (1986) describes the tutor's role in open learning programs as that of a facilitator and lists the following personal qualities which may need to be considered when selecting tutors:

- patient, tolerant and able to cope with frustration;
- perceptive (ability to put themselves in student's shoes), understanding, sympathetic
- friendly, approachable and trustworthy;
- prepared to tolerate disruption in private life;
- able to change quickly from one task or subject to another;
- prepared to accept interruptions to non-open tutor activity, eg lecturing.

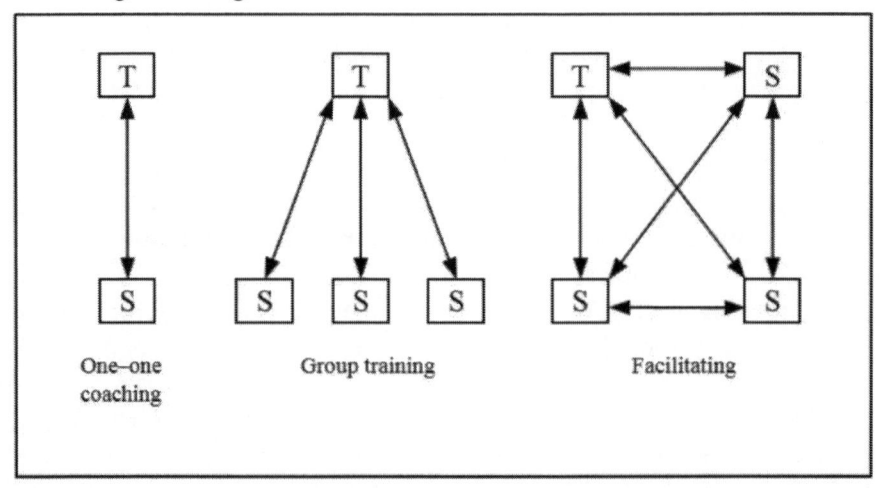

Figure 2.2   Traditional tutor roles compared with facilitating

It is not likely that all of the qualities presented by Rogers and by Clarke will be required of all facilitators in every learning situation. However, an assessment of the demands of the program will help to identify which qualities are relevant.

In addition to the selection and development of trainers as facilitators, some consideration must be given to the logistics of a training program which includes facilitative methods. More time may be required to allow for a number of the tactics, eg role-playing and discussions, to be exploited fully and for individual counseling. The size of the group may have to be reduced or more than one tutor may be needed so that syndicates can be formed. Experience has shown that when numbers are larger than eight, smaller syndicate groups are needed. More space is likely to be needed to cater for group and individual activity and possibly a resource bank of information and equipment. The functions and skills of the trainer or tutor which have been examined so far are those which involve direct contact with trainees. The skills and competencies of those who are involved in the design and presentation of open learning are of equal importance. Bhugra (1986) has identified the value of the use of 'creative teams'. In the context of computer-based training, the creative team relies upon the trainer to ensure that the analysis of behavior, the identification of training needs and the writing of terminal objectives, enabling objectives and learning points are carried out properly. Then the creative team of wordsmiths, a graphic artist and a coder can design the training. The role of the wordsmiths is to apply their skills in the use of the English language to ensure that the 'scripted' message is presented economically, accurately and simply. The graphic artist contributes the skills of layout, presentation, color, illustration and typeface, and the coder program the material. The team roles are not seen as discrete:

the wordsmiths edit material and graphic artists code their own graphics. The concept of a creative team is equally applicable to those trainers who are involved in the production of learning packages, training kits and job aids. They are all involved in the process of helping people to learn and must use appropriate skills and techniques which will substitute for those used by the face-to-face trainer. A considerable emphasis has been placed on the skills needed by trainers operating in different modes; however, theirs is not the only contribution which influences effective learning. Murray (1987) described how 'supporters' helped trainees in the glass industry to overcome problems with study techniques, the feeling of being abandoned and the difficulty of approaching tutors when they had problems. Supporters do not necessarily have to be subject experts; they make their contribution by taking an interest, checking progress, acting as a sounding board and giving encouragement. Murray indicated that those who gained most from open learning were those who received formal and informal follow-up from senior managers in their parent organizations. The responsibility of line managers must not be neglected when consideration is given to trainer skills. Apart from the fact that they have a managerial responsibility to ensure that their staff are trained and involved in develop- mental program, they may be involved in coaching activities and they should ensure that trainees are properly briefed before embarking on training program and that they are debriefed on its conclusion. Trainers who ensure that line managers appreciate the value of thorough briefing and who provide briefing guides for their use are often rewarded with better prepared and better motivated trainees entering the training program.

Changing roles of the trainer

The economic, technological, social and political context within which organizations are now required to operate is in a state of continual flux. It is imperative for them to adapt and adjust to or capitalize on these changes in order to flourish and survive. But to do so they must become, in Garrett's (1987) phrase, 'The Learning Organization'. If trainers are going to make a significant contribution to bringing this about and to effecting what, for many organizations, will be a major cultural shift in this respect, then they will have to adopt a different attitude to the nature and level of their own involvement in their organizations. Many of them will have to change:

- from being passive to being more active in communicating the benefits of training;
- from merely adopting a reactive response to taking on a more proactive stance in dealing with performance problems;
- from seeing themselves as peripheral, to perceiving themselves and the training function as central to and a key influence on the organization reaching its objectives;
- from simply being technologists, to developing a more strategic role; giving direction to the learning function and formulating training policy.

In other words, the roles trainers perform will have to expand to enable them to take their rightful place in human resource development. Bennett (1988) maintains that five key roles emerge from the various classifications he surveyed. Figure 2.3 shows the links and interrelationships between these classifications.

Trainer is mainly concerned with actually carrying out training, ie directly assisting the trainee to learn, supplying feedback, etc. This role may involve a variety of different training methods ranging from one-to-one instruction to project work.

Provider – designing, updating, maintaining and delivering training programs are the key functions of this role. More specifically the trainer would be involved in undertaking training needs analysis(es), establishing training objectives and possibly training or coaching trainers to deliver training.

Consultant – there are two main features to this role, analyzing organizational problems and then recommending solutions, that may require training. The more detailed activities include liaison with line managers, advising training managers on training aims, objectives and policies, etc.

Innovator – the primary concerns in this training role are supporting and assisting organizations to bring about effective change and to solve performance problems. These would involve the trainer in some of the following: working closely with middle and senior managers on change issues; identifying where learning and educational events, such as seminars and workshops, can help managers to understand and facilitate change; advising the training function as to its possible contribution to the change process.

Manager – in this role there is concern fundamentally with planning, organizing, controlling and developing the training function. In particular the manager sets training goals and formulates training policies and plans, liaises with other departments to show them the ways training can contribute to improving their employees' performance, ensuring and overseeing the development, delivery and evaluation of appropriate training activities, recruiting and developing training personnel, controlling activities against an overall training plan and budget.

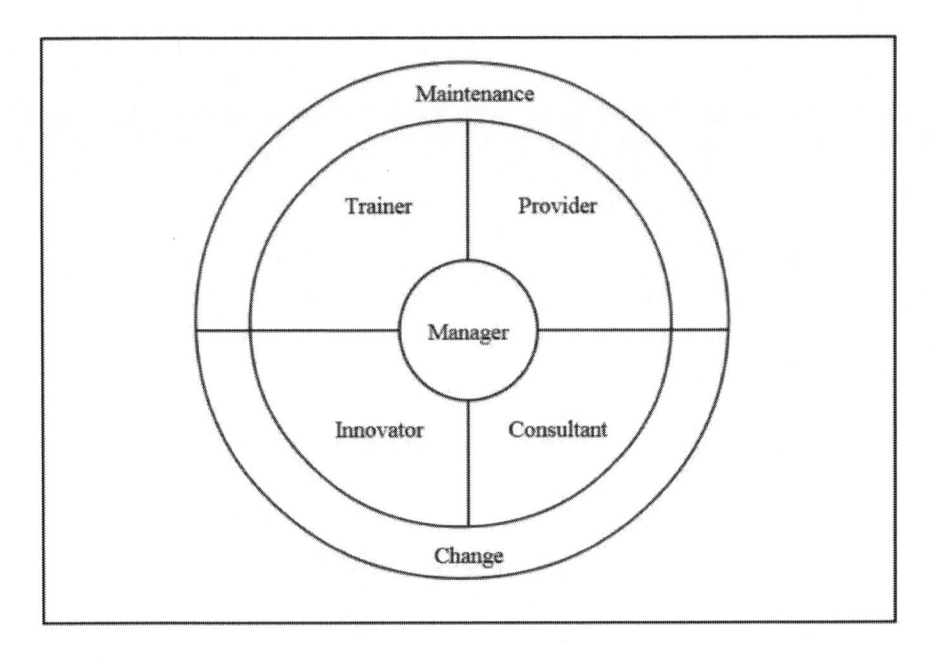

Figure 2.3 General trainer roles (Bennett, 1988)

In reality, the actual job of any trainer is probably going to contain elements from more than one of the above and, by virtue of its make-up, the manager's role is likely to be the common denominator. However, in the past and in a large number of organizations in the present, the emphasis has been or is on the trainer and provider roles. To be more influential, to command a higher profile in organizations and realize their full potential, trainers must move into the innovator and consultant modes.

The consultancy role of the trainer

The transition into the consultancy mode is of particular interest when considering the development of trainers. To be effective as a consultant the trainer must understand the main phases of the consulting model and acquire the appropriate knowledge, skills, attitudes and perspectives associated with each phase. Figure 2.4 is a model of training consultancy. It has nine main stages:

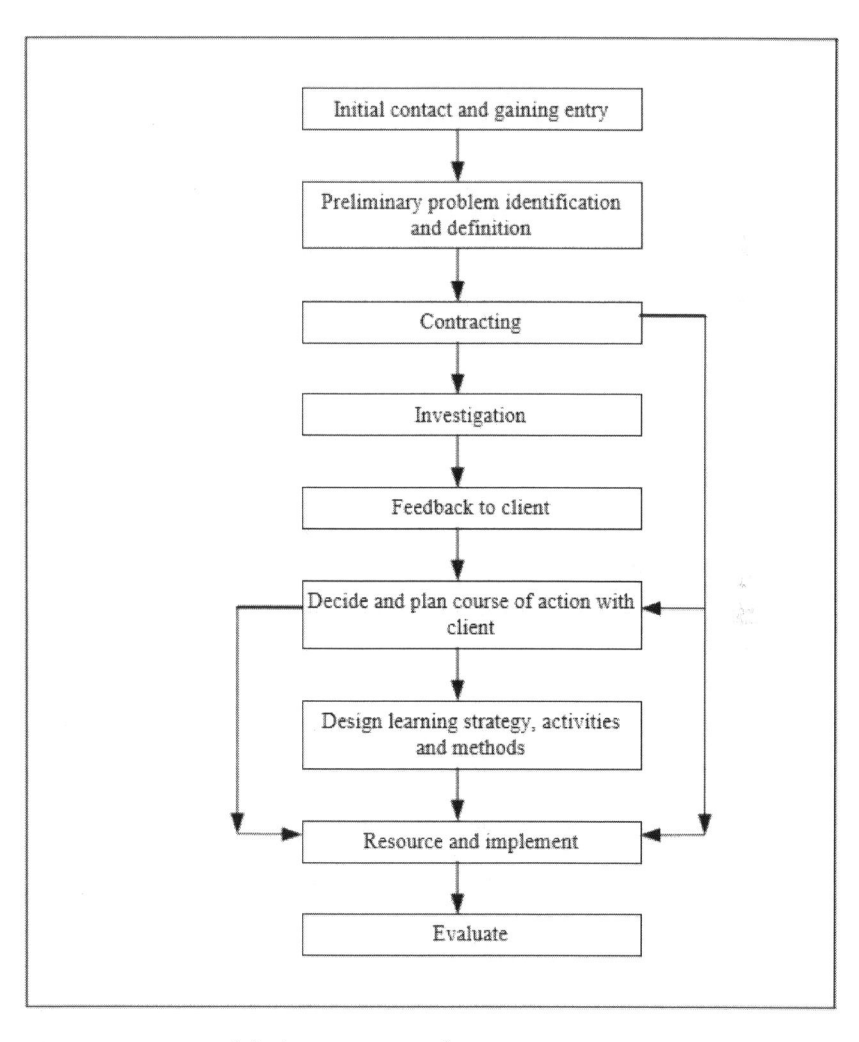

```
Initial contact and gaining entry
            ↓
Preliminary problem identification
        and definition
            ↓
         Contracting ←──────┐
            ↓               │
       Investigation        │
            ↓               │
     Feedback to client     │
            ↓               │
Decide and plan course of action with client ←──┐
            ↓                                    │
  Design learning strategy, activities           │
          and methods                            │
            ↓                                    │
     Resource and implement ←───────────────────┘
            ↓
         Evaluate
```

Figure 2.4 A model of training consultancy

> *Initial contact and gaining entry* – in organizations where training consultants or training consultancy services are well established, potential clients will often make the first contact. However, where trainers are developing their consultancy role they may want to take the initiative. There are a number of ways in which they may be able to gain access to managers including training course follow-up visits, mounting special marketing events, etc. Establishing rapport and credibility will be a major requirement of the consultant at this stage.

> *Preliminary problem identification and definition* – the training consultant should assist the client to articulate clearly his or her version of the nature of the problem or how the problem is perceived. In addition, the client should be helped to separate out symptoms from possible causes. The training consultant may need to persuade the client to allow him or her to undertake some preliminary enquiry in order to obtain a more secure database on which to take forward the discussion.

> *Contracting* – this involves the training consultant and client agreeing upon the terms of reference for the project or assignment that they feel is necessary bearing in mind what emerged at the previous stage. Constraints, resources, timescales, expectations and client involvement are issues to be considered and, if necessary, negotiated when drawing up a contract.

> *Investigation* – this entails designing and implementing the methodology for gathering further information about the problem. An attempt is made to pin down the cause or causes of the problem. In addition, possible solutions are generated and evaluated, ideally by both consultant and client.

> *Feedback to client* – findings, conclusions, interpretations and recommendations are presented to the client orally or

in writing. Although the consultant should be persuasive, overselling must be avoided. The consultant must maintain the involvement of the client, which should have been nurtured from the outset. If it has not been then there is a danger that the client will not feel a sense of ownership or commitment to proposals for future action.

➤ *Decide and plan course of action with client* – the consultant will need to analyze what contribution of training or learning initiative will be needed to resolve the problem. This may involve him or her in undertaking a new project or assignment for which a fresh contract will need to be agreed with the client. Agreement will also have to be reached at this stage about the criteria against which to evaluate the learning strategy that may be developed and implemented.

➤ *Design learning strategy, activities and methods* – the trainer consultant should consider learning strategies that go beyond, or even exclude, traditional training activities. Such strategies might include projects, self-directed workshops, team development and self-development groups.

➤ *Resource and implement* – with the client the consultant considers the resourcing implications of the agreed learning strategy. This may result in the training consultant helping the user organization, department or section to develop its own training resources. To cover this possibility further contracting may need to be undertaken at this point. In particular, if the learning activities are work-based the trainer consultant will have to be more flexible in the implementation of the learning strategy.

➤ *Evaluate* – this should be both in terms of learning and in organizational terms. The client and the 'trainees' must be intimately involved in this process. In addition the trainer consultant may also want to evaluate his or her own performance as a consultant, so that lessons can be carried forward to the next project (although feedback from the client should be sought throughout the consultancy process).

Adopting this model means that the trainer, as Holdaway and Saunders (1992) suggest, becomes less of a course provider and more of a diagnostician and problem resolver. As a training consultant, the trainer is likely to have to:

- work with the client manager, as an equal partner, in a collaborative way;
- provide training that is more tailored to the client's specific needs rather than simply presenting a set menu of courses or program;
- help trainees to acquire the skills of learning so that they become more responsible for, and more in control of, their own learning and development;
- operate, in many instances, at the workplace or 'in' the organization;
- train and develop line managers to become trainers and developers of others.

It is not always possible for trainers to undertake the consultancy role in full. There can be a number of reasons for this. Some consultancy projects could be time-consuming, trainers may have an existing heavy workload, the work may be of a sensitive nature or involve internal politics, or the subject matter could require specialist knowledge or techniques that the trainer does not have. Another reason which cannot always be justified is that the organization feels work undertaken by outside consultants has more credibility than that of an internal consultant. Sometimes this belief has proved to be costly. There is no doubt that using outside consultants has many advantages, but before such decisions are made it is worth considering the relative advantages and disadvantages of using internal and external consultancy.

| Advantages of internal consult- | Disadvantages of internal con- |

...ants	...sultants
The organizational structure and personalities are known	They may be regarded as too much a part of the organization.
The culture, language and politics of the organization are familiar.	They could face difficulties establishing credibility with senior management.
Gaining entry may be easier because of existing work relationships.	There is a danger of making assumptions or being biased by being too close to the problem or the organization.
There may be an existing network of contacts from which information and support can be sought.	Could they possibly be part of the problem?
An amount of information about the problem may be held already.	Their status could make it difficult to challenge people, policies and practices.
They can work unobtrusively and take opportunities to observe by being in situ	It could be difficult to gain access to some key players, especially those in senior positions.
They can monitor progress closely.	They could have political or hierarchical pressures applied to favor specific outcomes.
They are well placed to support implementation of outcomes	The project could be treated superficially through lack of time or specialist knowledge
They are in a position to implement strategies to evaluate the project.	
They may be more cost-effective.	
They can identify appropriate and inappropriate reasons for bringing in external consultants.	

Advantages of external consultants	Disadvantages of external consultants
They are seen as impartial and independent of influences of the	They may need more time than can be afforded to learn about the

organization.	organization.
They are regarded as having credibility through being independent.	They may have only sufficient time to identify and explore part of the problem
Their involvement may highlight the problem and promote greater involvement of key players.	Recommendations may be accepted too readily.
They can have wide access within the organization	Recommendations may be rejected if they are considered to be too radical for the organization.
They can be more challenging and direct and cut through entrenched views and practices.	Contracted time may expire before the recommendations are implemented fully
People are more likely to be open in their contributions and trust that they are given in confidence.	They may encourage the client to become dependent on outside consultancy services.
They can open communication channels across the organization	The costs of external consultancy are high and visible.
They can introduce new ideas and draw upon a wide experience of different organizations.	
They can provide networking and benchmarking with other organizations.	
There is often a greater acceptance of recommendations from outside.	

Marketing the training function

It cannot be ignored that, in some organizations, training does not appear to be held in such high esteem as other functions. There are historical precedents which have made this understandable up to a point. However, as the role of the trainer has changed and trainers have developed their skills and expertise to meet these changes, the training department has become a more potent resource, and one which has the potential to make significant contributions to the success of an organization.

Although this has been recognized in most organizations, there remains a need for trainers to maintain a high profile, highlight their successes and encourage those who ignore or merely pay lip service to the training function to make better use of what is on offer. There have been many instances of the expertise of the training department being overlooked as a result of initiatives such as empowerment, which has given line managers the opportunity to make their own decisions about training needs and how they can be met. However, not all line managers have the necessary skills or experience to identify needs accurately, or the necessary knowledge to be able to select the most appropriate form of training or the most appropriate provider. It is against this kind of background that trainers have to market their expertise and the services they have to offer. Very often it is the reactions of former trainees that influence line managers' decisions about the value and effectiveness of training, and their perception of the training function. Image is the key factor in marketing, and the training function needs to be proactive in promoting that image and not leave it to chance. This proactivity includes being involved whenever there is a change to the organizational structure, when business plans are written or reviewed, and when there are changes to the staff and the skills and knowledge that they require. In order to achieve this it is important to identify the key players, the decision makers and those who hold the 'purse strings' within the organization, and to become their advisor on all matters relating to training and development. In developing this relationship manager role, a large proportion of time needs to be given to listening. That involves listening not only to those in the power positions but to line managers and to staff, and showing them that the training function is able to meet the need, and that the training can be structured and delivered in a way that suits them. In some cases the training function may not be able to meet the need from its own resources but it should be able to offer outside providers or recommend alternative forms of learning. By offering such a service, it helps to develop a system by which all training and development issues are channeled through the training function. However, this only works if the training function and those in it have the respect and confidence of line managers. This is down to image. First imprisons really do count, and trainers need to give careful and deliberate consideration to how they want to be seen by all of those who become involved with them. One might expect such words as 'professional', 'well organized' and 'responsive' to be included. It is easy to make a list but it is more demanding to limit that list to four or five key descriptors, and then to develop and implement strategies and guidelines to ensure that the desired image is created and maintained. The majority of effective trainers apply such image-creating practices as a matter of course. The pride that they have in their professionalism makes it common sense to them, but it is worth giving some consideration to these practices from the marketing perspective. They include:

Appearance. All members of the team should look smart and be alert. They should be responsive, welcoming and supportive. The manner in which telephone calls are dealt with, the way in which visitors are treated, the way in which training is delivered and the way in which participation in meetings is exercised have a great impact on image.

Punctuality. Training sessions should begin on time and as far as is practical the timings for sessions should be adhered to. Even though some trainees may be late, the trainer should always be in attendance. Being on time for meetings and appointments is equally important, and a prompt follow-up letter or memorandum to summarize what has been discussed or decided underlines the efficiency of the trainer.

Administrative procedures. Standard administrative procedures should be drawn up in such a way that all of the training team are familiar with them and are in a position to advise or initiate them when needed. These include receipt and confirmation of nominations for courses, booking rooms and catering.

Correspondence. A standard format for letters, memoranda, e-mail, joining instructions etc should be used by the whole team.

Training facilities. The appearance of the training facilities is as important as personal appearance. It is accepted that in many cases the training function is not allocated the best of accommodation. However, a clean environment which is free of broken and unwanted furniture, together with appropriate seating arrangements and an uncluttered well laid-out training room, goes a long way to compensate.

Training materials. As with correspondence, items such as handouts, exercises, pre-course material, OHP/PowerPoint slides, and questionnaires should conform to a house style which identifies the material with the training function. They should be neat, well designed and up-to-date.

Packaging. Ring binders or files for course material should be of an appropriate size for what they have to contain. An attractive and well-designed cover or front sheet, particularly one that indicates the material has been designed to meet the needs of a specific group, shows that special attention has been given to them.

Learning strategies. Activities such as role-play, discussion, case study and syndicate work need to be supported with clear and specific guidelines. The management of these activities demands close monitoring, intervention when direction is lost, and realistic allocation of time so that the exercises are actually completed and debriefed.

Language level. In addition to an appropriate level of language being used in written materials and in the delivery of training, it is important to ensure that in meetings everyone understands what the trainer is talking about. Senior managers are not impressed by the use of technical terms they do not understand.

Advertising. Keeping training 'in the public eye' should be an ongoing activity. It has been suggested already that trainers should become involved in meetings and events at organizational level. In addition, trainers can make use of house journals to promote training by submitting articles, success stories and course reviews by former students, photographs, details of forthcoming training events etc. The training function may be able to produce its own newsletter or make use of an intranet to promote its role. Offering to speak at meetings to update senior staff on trends, achievements and the results of evaluation exercises may also be of value.

Staffing. In order to maintain the image the training function wants, staff should be selected who will help to uphold that image. It is to be expected that they are sufficiently qualified for the role to have credibility, and that provision is made for them to receive further training and to develop their skills and knowledge.

This list is not intended to be exhaustive, and experienced trainers will be able to add to it. Its intention is to focus on a few critical areas so that those damaging nightmare scenarios do not occur.

Stuart and Long believe that this marketing orientation is, in some areas of training, preferable to the production, sales, finance and people orientations which they describe in fairly critical terms. A summary of what these orientations involve is set out below:

Production orientation There is in this orientation an over-emphasis on the absolute quality of the service being offered. Obsessive concerns with detail, high development and design costs, inflexibility of program, and trainer rather than learner centeredness characterize this approach.

Sales orientation not surprisingly selling the product, without necessarily emphasizing the quality, is at the root of this approach. 'Bottoms on seats' is the overriding consideration with learning outcomes and appropriateness taking very much a 'back seat'.

Finance orientation Cost is the major factor influencing the training decision in this approach and not effectiveness of learning. Although cutting back on costs is often the main concern of a trainer working within this orientation, ironically on some occasions the converse may be true. There are trainers who think good training must be expensive or seen to be expensive. 'Never mind the quality look at the width' or 'An ounce of image is worth a pound of performance' are sentiments which often motivate both the finance and sales-orientated training function.

People orientation This orientation might be retitled self-orientation. The trainers produce programs more in line with their own interests than those of their potential clients. Such interests may be rather esoteric and 'progressive' and consequently divorced from matters of particular every- day relevance.

Ethics and the trainer

Drawing heavily on the British Psychological Society's 'Code of Ethics and Conduct' (2006) and the authors' extensive experience, set out below are ways in which trainers must or should ethically handle some of the key considerations they may face:

- *Record Keeping*: collect and maintain appropriate and accurate records consistent with professional purposes and legal requirements.
- *Confidentiality*: do not disclose details of client organizations or of trainees to other parties, internal or external, unless there is a legal obligation to do so or legitimate authority has been given.
- *Copyright*: attribute theories and models referred to in handouts and in training sessions to the correct originators and not take credit for ideas produced by others and not plagiarize or neglect to acknowledge the work or contribution of others.
- *Research Authenticity:* report accurately and fully research results that inform or impinge on training activities.
- *Personal Competence and Development*: maintain and develop their knowledge and skills by undertaking some form of Continuing Professional Development, possibly through membership of a professional body.

- *Training Material*: keep training material used on programs and assignments current and up-to-date.
- *Provide Value for Money*: use appropriate resources and, unless there are sound professional or economic reasons, not show favor to particular providers, locations, etc.
- *Financial Probity*: manage any financial matters honestly and not seek to gain any pecuniary advantage through the training or consultancy activity undertaken by offering trainees or client's financial inducements in order to obtain future work or favor's.
- *Honesty*: provide accurate information about self, qualifications and experience; not make claims about their expertise that are unjustified.
- *Off-the-Shelf Programs*: do not take an off-the-shelf programs and claim that it is tailor-made.
- *Sensitivity*: be alert to a trainee's needs, abilities, disabilities and difficulties, and to cultural and ethnic differences in relation to the content of and methods of training employed.
- *Objectivity*: give trainees or clients honest and objective feedback about training performance or organizational research results at appropriate times and in a manner that respects their integrity and sensitivities.
- *Compliance* – comply with relevant legislation on equal opportunities, human rights and how these relate to training.
- *Relationships with Trainees*: do not develop intimate or personal relationships, including sexual, with trainees, clients or colleagues during the course of a training program or assignment as this may adversely affect outcomes and relationships.
- *'Shop' Fellow Professionals*: do not turn a 'blind eye' and be prepared to inform on fellow professionals or others if they do not respond in a constructive way to advice to desist from performing or behaving in an unethical fashion.
- *Consistency:* behave consistently over time and towards different trainees by not showing favoritism, as this may

unfavorably affect group morale and give one or several trainees an unfair advantage.
- *Codes of Conduct* – establish clear codes of conduct and behavior at the outset of and during the course of a training event or assignment and adhere to and not contradict or ignore these codes.
- *Realism:* do not raise unrealistic expectations about what a training course or program can achieve with trainees or clients.

I know that now you are saying it's impossible to keep all that!

It's not impossible it's hard we are all humans not angles none of us are sin free! But try as much as you can, and remember trainees always look up to you and will not question the information you provide them.

Chapter 4: Learning Principles and Conditions

So we talked in the previous chapters about training within an organization, trainer roles, ethic's...etc

Let's talk about the core of the training which is learning process. In choosing or developing your own instructional methods based on the learning style of the trainees at hand. The purpose of this chapter is to provide brief information about learning principles and conditions.

Sequencing the training material

As we all know the "law" of information sequencing is easy to medium to complex, the training material must have some logical order you cannot start with medium to unknown to easy!

However to provide an accurate sequencing for the trainees you must do a pre-knowledge quiz, analyze the results that way you will know exactly the amount of information each trainee holds and how to sequence your training material. But keep in mind that there may a variation between each trainee in the amount of knowledge they hold or learning style.

Readiness of the learner

From the intellectual perspective the trainer already should have assessed the trainees' level of prerequisite knowledge and skill, general potential capability or special aptitudes relating to the intended training content. This will have been done through a review of the trainees' educational and occupational background or through the application of diagnostic or psychological tests. For example, engineering trainees might have been expected to demonstrate mechanical and spatial aptitudes to a reasonable level before embarking on their training, whereas for commercial apprentices verbal, clerical and numerical aptitudes might have been seen as more appropriate. However, intellectually, the trainees bring more to the training situation than simply their general or specific abilities to learn the material presented. Past training and educational experiences may have assisted them to learn how to learn, that is, to acquire learning strategies that enable them to assimilate new subject matter and develop skills more readily.

Downs and Perry (1982, 1984) have established short training courses to help trainees to improve their capacity to learn how to learn. In one of their program young trainees were introduced to exercises which were designed to improve generally their ability in memorization, in under- standing and in doing things.

In another training workshop for supervisors, who were responsible for carrying out training, a checklist of some of the dos and don'ts for improving learning to learn skills was developed and it is reproduced in Figure 2.5 to give a flavor of what Downs and Perry are advocating.

Do Show that all your trainees have a contribution to make	**By** Making sure that you take notice of their views
Don't Make things too easy	**By** Doing the difficult parts for the trainees
Do Make them seek help when they need it	**By** Not rushing in with help too soon
Don't Do it for them when they ask for help but encourage them to work it out for themselves	**By** Giving them clues or hints
Do Encourage trainees to identify and correct their own mistakes	**By** Providing models and guiding them with questions
Don't Make the learning too easy	**By** Breaking it into small parts. Get them to break it up for themselves
Do Allow them time to work something out for themselves	**By** Giving them pondering time. If they feel pushed for time, they may become stressed
Don't Give unrealistic feedback	**By** Giving undue praise or overcritical comment
Do Develop the trainees' interest in learning to do things for themselves	**By** Discussing with them how they intend to go about learning something
Don't Belittle your trainees' attempts at learning	**By** Laughing at them or comparing them unkindly with others
Do Develop the trainees' awareness of how to assess what they have done	**By** Getting them to check their own work and assess it for quality
Don't Give tasks which are too easy or too hard	**By** Selecting a task which is inappropriate to their previous experience
Do Make your trainees realize that practising is necessary for both consolidating learning and gaining skill	**By** Encouraging them to do things a number of times giving careful attention to any mistakes they make

Figure 2.5 some dos and don'ts for developing learning skills (Downs and Perry, 1984)

Motivation can be defined here as that which energizes, directs and sustains behavior or performance. There are a number of factors that will influence whether or not this 'active, purposive and goal-directed behavior' is forthcoming. To assist with the identification of the most important of these factors and to aid the general discussion on motivation in the training context, reference will be made to a model of motivation illustrated in Figure 2.6 The first feature of this model that must concern the trainer relates to the trainees' needs. Such needs can be classified under the following headings:

Physical	sexual, nutritional
Safety	support, security
Emotional: individual	control, independence, achievement, self-confidence, challenge, autonomy, approval
Emotional: social	acceptance, recognition, respect, status, appreciation, belonging
Intellectual	curiosity, variety, stimulation
Self-actualization	self-development, meaning, sense of purpose

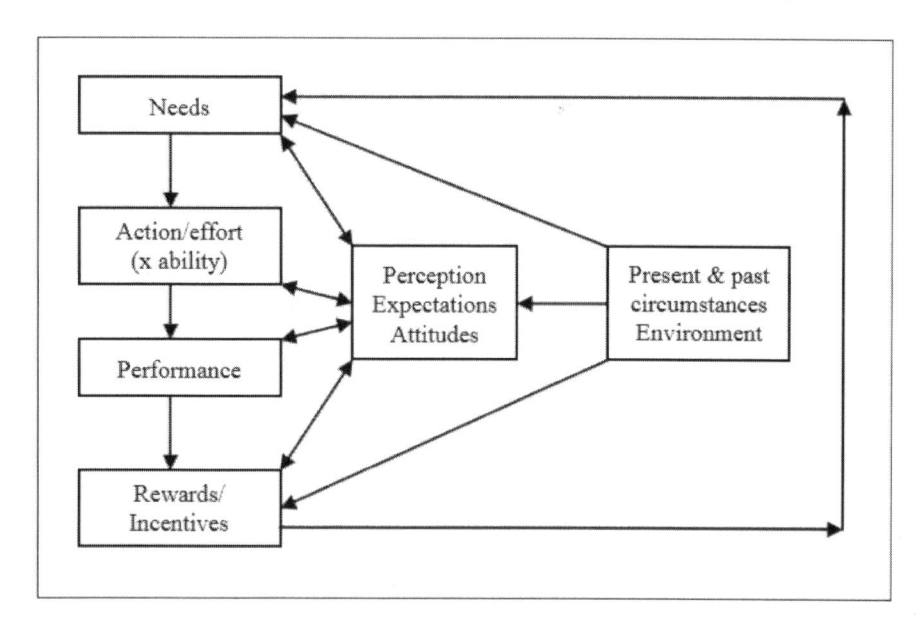

Figure 2.6 Model of motivation

Ways of learning

Why do people learn? How do people learn? Well there are 5 common ways that people learn and why people learn is basically a human activities that we perform in order to survive and develop.

Trial and error

The simplest form of learning. The learner acts or behaves with the intention of achieving some result or end state. Each action that is perceived as leading towards this desired outcome is reinforced and, all things being equal, will be repeated on subsequent occasions. If a particular action or behavior meets with a lack of success, or even punishing consequences, it is unlikely to be repeated and the learner then 'searches' for an appropriate alternative. By a series of trials, approximations and errors the learner may eventually discover the correct sequence of action.

Perceptual organization

The learner perceives the total stimulus situation – cues, conditions, rewards, etc – and then organizes it or 'maps it out' into a comprehensible or understand- able pattern that guides or directs his or her behavior.

Behavior modeling

A great deal of human learning is a result of first observing how others have behaved, and have been rewarded or punished in particular situations, and then by attempting to imitate the correct or most appropriate performance or series of behaviors.

Mediation

Language, in oral or written form, is an intermediary or meditational process through which human beings acquire a great deal of what they learn during their lifetime. The communication or language code may not only be in words but also in the form of symbols, diagrams or figures.

Reflection

This way of learning is closely associated with perceptual organization and may, in many cases, follow on from trial and error, behavior modeling or mediation. It is, as Boot and Boxer (1980) point out, 'a process of thinking back on, reworking, searching for meanings in experience' or, as Boud, Keogh and Walker (1985) suggest, 'an active process of exploration and discovery' which involves 'thinking quietly, mulling over and making sense of experience'.

General conditions of learning

The trainer must engage the trainee in the learning process in an active fashion. Before examining some of the specific actions the trainee and the trainer may need to take in order to fulfill this requirement, attention must be paid to the general conditions of learning within the training situation that either positively promote, or are conducive to, learning. As many experienced trainers have learned, fall-off in attention can be minimized by employing visual aids, varying pitch, pace and tone of voice, changing physical position, introducing humor and varying the activity of the groups. In self-study activities such as programmed learning, computer- based training, e-learning or the use of learning packages there is the likelihood of a similar fall-off period. In addition to interacting with the medium of instruction, it is helpful for trainees to have the opportunity to interact with their tutors, other trainees and supervisors to share problems, seek assistance and confirm progress which contributes to increasing their attention level.

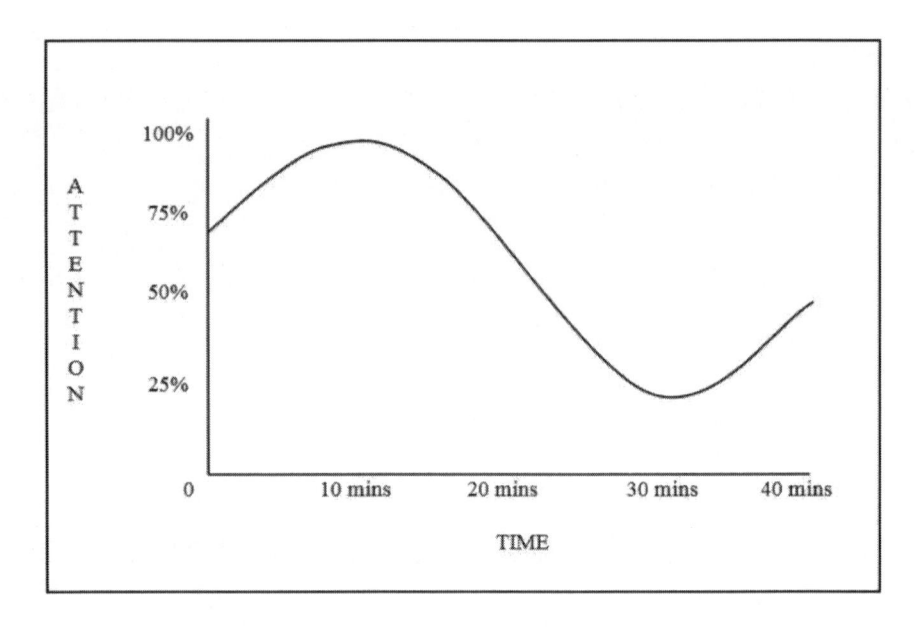

Figure 2.7 Group attention over time (after Mills, 1967)

By continually demonstrating the significance of content through credible and relevant examples the trainer should go some way to maintaining the trainees' interest.

The traditional recommendation that new material should be covered in the morning and early afternoon periods and then consolidated in the afternoon period has been complicated and brought into question by recent research. Certainly, immediate retention generally appears to be better in the earlier part of the day. However, longer term retention (Folkard, 1987) for some tasks may be higher following presentation in the afternoon and evening. There may be several explanations for this seemingly surprising finding:

- Trainers recognize the onset of the mental 'dip' and make greater effort to stimulate trainees.
- Trainees perceive a diminution in their attentiveness and put more effort into concentrating on the training material.
- Certain groups are predisposed towards more effective performance later on in the day.

There are 'morning' and 'evening' types. The former wake earlier and become fully operational mentally fairly quickly but tend to tire relatively early in the evening period. The 'evening' types are the converse; they are slow to get into mental action but can stay up much later at night, and remain reasonably alert.

Not to deny the above possibilities, Folkard (1987) nevertheless suggests that with regard to time of day effects in performance research findings on task demands and individual differences make it difficult to recommend the best time for scheduling work over the course of the normal day. Although it is known that task demands affect performance trends, specific recommendations cannot as yet be made about the best time of day to undertake most tasks. In the absence of evidence to the contrary, it would seem that this conclusion could also apply to training. However, where does this leave the trainer on the problem of the timing of learning input? Possibly the most sensible suggestions for the trainer to follow are:

- Irrespective of the nature of the target population, over the course of the day, look to vary the training methods employed.
- Build into the training program 'natural' breaks, rest periods and relaxation 'slots'
- Be keenly aware of the potential problem of input 'overload' particularly with lower ability groups and those who have been out of training and education for some time.
- Build in reinforcement strategies.

Principles and specific conditions supporting learning

Besides considering how the training material should best be sequenced the trainer must also think carefully about another important organizing issue, namely whether or not to cover what has to be learned as a whole or in parts. For instance, when the task has several elements, should they be learned all at once or should the trainee be taught the elements separately, before combining them into the whole? The answer to this question seems to be 'it depends'. Baldwin and Ford (1988) in their literature review suggest that the whole method is more advantageous when the learner has high intelligence, when practice on the task is distributed rather than massed (see below) and when the learning material is high in task organization but low in task complexity (task organization refers to the degree to which sub-tasks or task elements are interrelated). Goldstein (1986) deviates to an extent from the views of Baldwin and Ford. Interpreting the examination of the literature on whole versus part learning by Naylor (1962) and Blum and Naylor (1968) the following training principles are supported:

> When a task has relatively high organization, an increase in task complexity leads to whole methods being more efficient than part methods, and when a task has low organization, an increase in task complexity leads to part methods being more efficient.

Goldstein emphasizes the importance of analyzing the task in order to deter- mine whether it can be split up easily into coherent parts. In addition, he suggests that the analysis may indicate that a form of progression learning could be usefully adopted. There are a number of options that can be used:

Progressive part, where the first two parts of the task are practiced in isolation and are then practiced together. The third part is practiced in isolation and then added to the first two parts and so on. eg A, B, A+B, C, A+B+C etc

Repetitive part, sometimes known as cumulative part, where the first part of the task is practiced in isolation and then the second and subsequent parts added. eg A, A+B, A+B+C etc

Isolated part, where some of the parts of the task are practiced in isolation before the whole task is practiced. eg A, C, E, A+B+C+D+E etc

Retrogressive part, where the last part of the task is practiced in isolation, then the last and the penultimate part, and so on until the whole task has been learned. eg C, B, A, A+B+C

If training is to be adaptive and managed flexibly then it is important for the trainer to monitor carefully the progress of individual trainees over an appropriate period of time. Where it is practicable to do so, the construction of learning curves could be of major assistance in this endeavor. Learning curves are a way of describing the changes in performance brought about by training and take the form of a graph tracing the improvement, or otherwise, of trainees during the course of the training program. The general benefits of learning curves are:

- Provide diagnostic information that may help the trainer to determine the effectiveness of the training tactics and methods employed
- Used to give feedback to the trainee.
- Alert the trainer to difficulties being experienced by the trainees as indicated by slow progress or no progress being made.

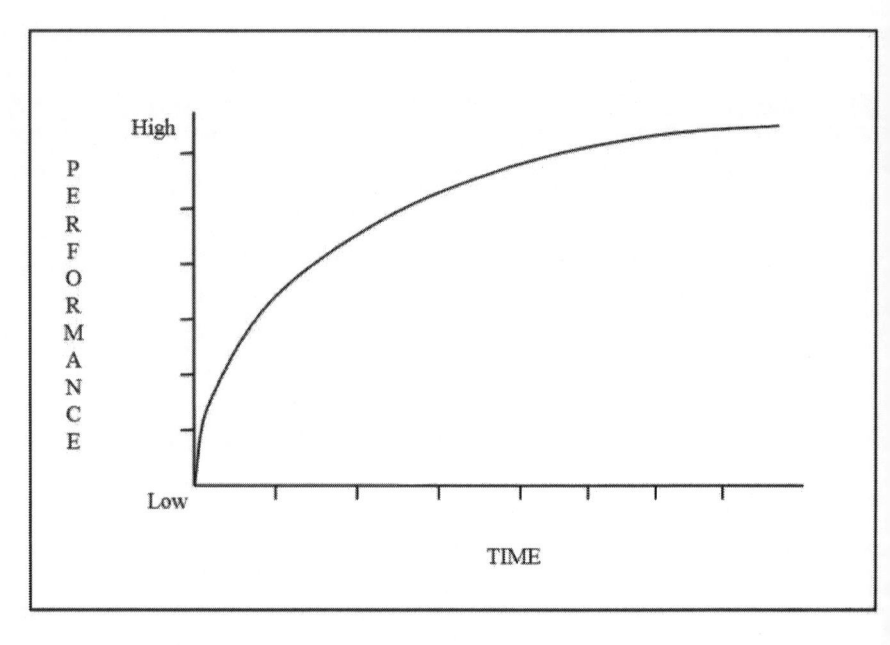

Figure 2.8 Negatively accelerated learning curve

Several reasons have been put forward to explain the development of this pattern of performance:

- The task to be learned is reasonably easy and therefore dramatic initial progress is possible.
- The trainee's previous learning experience enables him or her to organize the new material in a meaningful way fairly quickly.
- The trainee may be highly motivated to start with but then begins to lose interest, particularly if the task is simple and straightforward.
- The basic task is essentially easy to learn and, at the beginning, a high quality outcome is not required.

To combat the effects of these influences the trainer may need to pay greater attention to the trainee towards the back end of the training either by supplying more accurate and more specific feedback or by being more encouraging in order to 'lift' the trainee's motivation or by introducing temporarily some stimulating alternative activity so that the trainee may return to the main task refreshed.

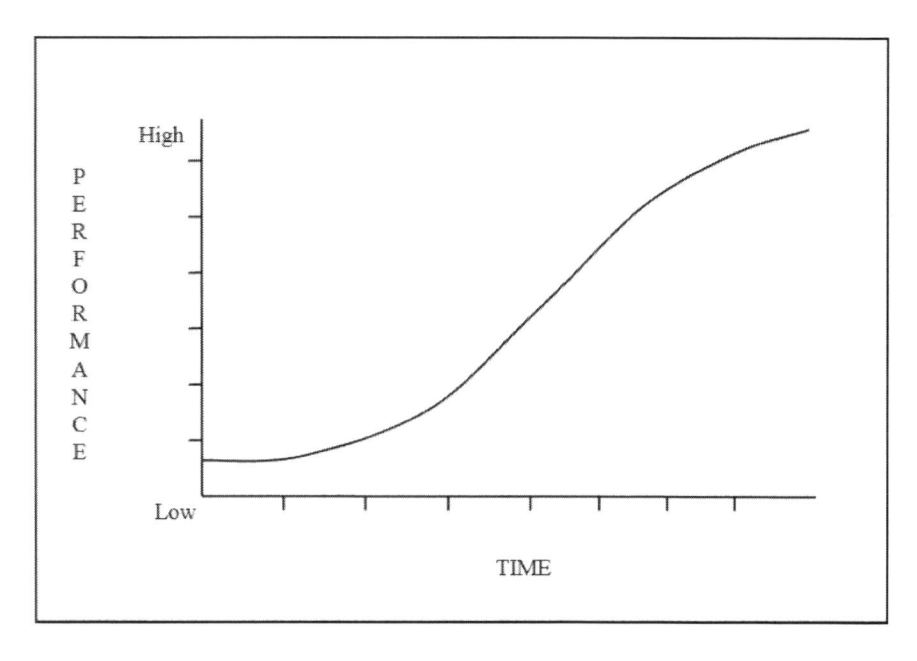

Figure 2.9 Positively accelerated learning curve

The second curve (Figure 2.9) is the converse of the first. This type of curve is usually associated with very difficult and complex training material and, where the trainee does not have the requisite experiential or educational background or special aptitudes to 'pick it up' quickly. Not surprisingly, the trainees' motivation also may be fairly low in the initial stages which further serve to depress their performance. In these circumstances the trainer probably will need to give more guidance and encouragement early on.

Transfer of training is an issue, sometimes a problem, closely associated with forgetting and skill loss. It occurs whenever the existence of a previously established habit or skill has an influence on the acquisition, performance or relearning of another habit or skill. In the training context positive transfer will have taken place if the trainee is able to apply on the job what has been learned in training with relative ease or is able to learn a new task more quickly as a result of earlier training on another task. Conversely negative transfer arises when performance on the job or on the new task is decelerated or hindered by what knowledge and skills have been acquired. Changing from a conventionally geared car to an automatic illustrates potential transfer problems. In this situation a number of skills learned on the conventional vehicle are likely to transfer positively to the automatic vehicle, such as steering, general road sense, etc, whereas to begin with gear changing and foot controls might be awkward to apply and not synchronize particularly well because of negative transfer.

Two sets of ideas or theories have been put forward to explain the transfer phenomenon and these have different implications for training. The theories have been referred to as the identical-elements theory and the transfer-through- principles theory. Figure 3.0 helps to explain and illustrate these two theories. The identical-elements theory claims that the nature of the transfer that takes place will depend on the degree to which there are common or identical stimulus and response elements in the training and work situations. If the stimulus conditions (ST/SW) and response requirements (RT/RW) in the environments of training and work are very similar, then there should be high positive transfer. Some forms of on-the-job training come close to fulfilling this kind of specification and this is the reason, no doubt, why this form of training can prove to be very effective. The opposite case, where the stimulus conditions and response requirements are totally dissimilar, would normally lead to no transfer at all. This kind of training scenario is highly improbable and, should it occur, would naturally raise very serious questions about the competence of the trainer or whoever undertook the training analyses and program design. Similar reservations about the trainer might be appropriate in the case of negative transfer; this is likely to occur where the stimulus situations are much the same or similar but the response requirements are different. The displays or equipment used in training may be or may look similar to what is used in the work situation. However, minor modifications or subtle alterations which have not been noted by, or communicated to, the trainer could have changed the response requirements to a significant degree. The trainees' on-the-job work performance will be affected directly. The work of others also may be disrupted and time may be wasted while the trainee learns new and more relevant responses. Finally, what happens when ST and SW are dissimilar but RT and RW are the same? The answer to this question would seem to be – it depends. If ST and SW are quite different then no transfer should take place, because the trainee will not associate SW with RW which is identical to RT and therefore will not respond appropriately when SW occurs. However, as ST and SW move closer together then provided there are common critical elements in these conditions positive transfer should result.

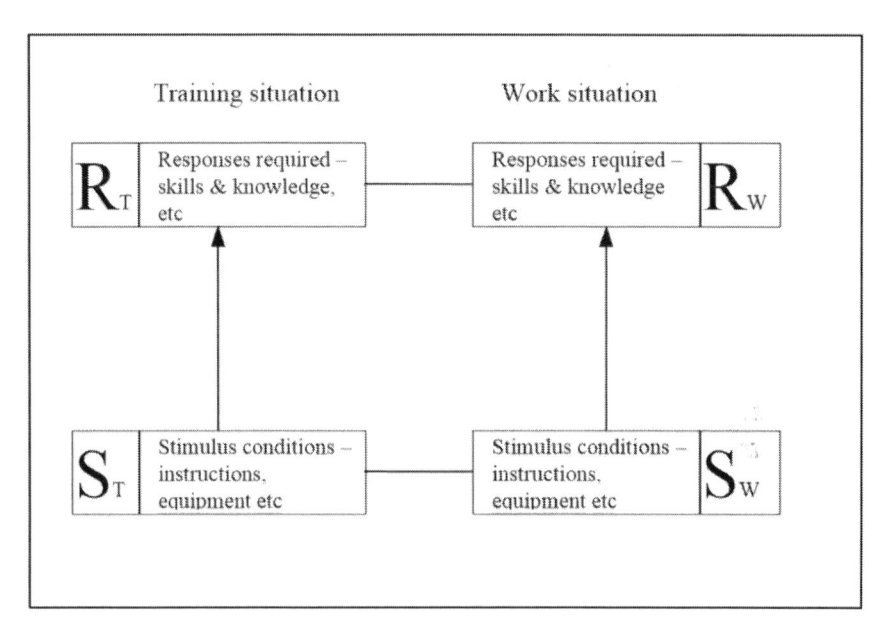

Figure 3.0 The identical-elements theory and the transfer-through-principles theory

Baldwin and Ford (1988) make two other suggestions to assist transfer, namely 'buddy systems' and 'booster sessions'. Buddy systems involve two trainees being paired off to work together post-training and to give one another mutual support, provide advice and be alert for signs of relapse in themselves and the buddy. Booster sessions are basically an extension of the original training with trainer and trainee meeting face-to-face for some kind of revision input period.

The principles, conditions and features of learning which have been covered so far are not all equally relevant to the kinds of material that could be included in a training session. Figure 3.1 sets out those which generally are most applicable to the different categories of training objective Gagné and Briggs (1979) describe a more complex and more detailed scheme for linking learning categories and conditions that would further assist trainers in their efforts to design and develop training programs. However, irrespective of what scheme is employed, it is vital for trainers to appreciate this critical point; the programs they establish, in order to realize particular types of training objective, must take clear account of and incorporate the learning principles and conditions that relate to those objectives. The relevant principles and conditions must be an integral part of the methods chosen or designed to achieve the stated objectives.

Training objective	Learning principles and conditions
Knowledge:	
Memorization	-Meaningful context
	-Accurate and immediate feedback
	-Prompting Rehearsal (retrieval)
	-Distributed practice
Comprehension	-Verbal introduction
	-Meaningful context
	- Rehearsal and feedback
	-Reflection
	-Distributed practice (reviews)
Skills:	
Intellectual	-Verbal introductions
	-Demonstration
	- Guidance, cueing and feedback
	- Practice – whole/part regime
	- Discovery learning
	- Reflection
Manual	-Demonstration
	-Practice – distributed
	-Feedback, guidance and cueing

	-Explanation
Social	-Over-learning
	-Verbal introductions
	-Human model
	-Practice Feedback, guidance and cueing
	-Imagining and reflection
Attitudes:	-Observation of human model
	-reinforcement (action taken)

Figure 3.1 Training objectives, learning principles and conditions

In Kolb's opinion the learning process can be reduced to two primary bipolar dimensions, incorporating the four learning modes outlined above. One of these dimensions is described by concrete experience at one pole and abstract conceptualization at the other, whereas the polar opposites of the other dimensions are active experimentation and reflective observation. Learning consists of moving in varying degrees between these opposite modes. Kolb suggests that individuals' choices of experience will influence which modes of learning are emphasized and which learning strategy or strategies they develop. Learning strategies involve combinations of basic learning modes, ie CE/RO, RO/AC, AE/CE/RO, etc. Kolb suggests that it is the combination of all four of these elementary learning forms that produces the highest level of learning. In Kolb's schema the learning styles that he has identified relate to pair combinations of the basic learning modes or abilities:

- Convergent style – the individual emphasizes the learning abilities of abstract conceptualization and active experimentation and shows strength in the practical application of ideas and problem solving.
- Divergent style – concrete experience and reflective observation abilities characterize individuals showing this style. Being imaginative and seeing things from many perspectives would describe people in this category.

- Assimilation style – the learning abilities of abstract conceptualization and reflective observation are dominant in a person adopting this style. Inductive reasoning and the ability to encompass disparate observations into an integrated framework are particular strengths of individuals displaying this style.
- Accommodative style – emphasis is placed on concrete experience and active experimentation abilities. The person adopting this style gets things done and gets involved in new experiences. Intuition and trial-and-error rather than theory are the basis for problem solving.

Kolb does not conceive learning styles as fixed personality traits but rather as adaptive orientations influenced by an individual's basic psychological make- up or type, educational specialization, career, present job and the specific task or problem the person is currently tackling. The foregoing discussion emphasizes that Honey and Mumford, and Kolb attach a great deal of importance to learning from experience. However, Caple and Martin (1994) find that there are a number of criticisms and questions that could be raised and observations made about their ideas, which may have implications for the usefulness of these ideas in a training context.

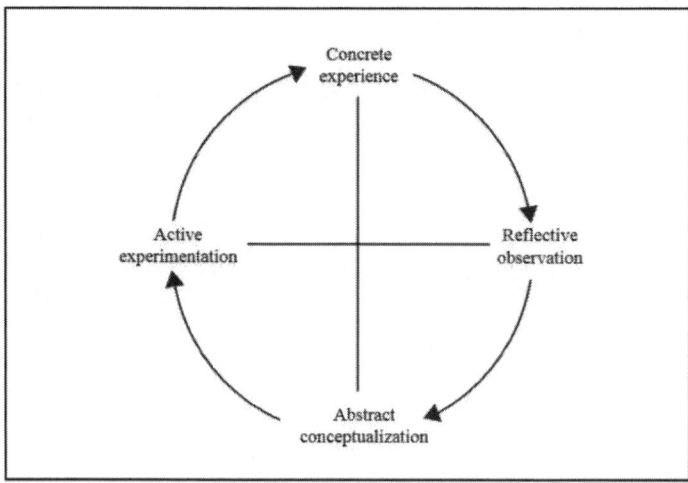

Figure 3.2 The learning cycle – Kolb

Chapter 5: What Is a Competency

Competencies are based on what a person does; they are behavioral and observable. If one is competent, then the result is effective or possibly out- standing job performance. A set of competencies is referred to as a competency model and is a collection of behaviors supported by underlying knowledge, skills, and attitudes that relate to a specific role or job responsibility. Building a competency model requires identifying a successful performance for a role or job responsibility and then defining the knowledge, skills, and attitudes that relate to that performance.

Competency models can and do vary from one organization to another, since success is most often defined in terms of meeting a business need. Business needs differ, so competency models differ. Common themes can be found in similar roles, regardless of the industry or business need. Training and development competencies across industries and businesses also vary due to differing business needs and the organization's purpose. When considering a competency model in a specific organization, it is helpful to look at the broadest variety of behaviors, knowledge, skills, and attitudes to create your own model.

How Competencies Are Built from Knowledge and Skill

The Competency Model (Figure 3.3) is circular because a variety of knowledge, skills, and attitudes support the agreed-on behaviors and performance. Behaviors and performance can be used in any role or responsibility to create a competency model. An example of a competency for a person with a job that includes a trainer's role is "the ability to set an adult learning climate." When selecting a competency, be sure to identify the role first. In this example, the role is a trainer. However, a course designer might also design session starters to set an adult learning climate. Next, describe the behavior; list the expected results or outputs; and identify supporting knowledge, skills, and attitudes. Provide separate descriptions for basic and advanced competencies. The following examples are a linear description of the basic climate-setting competency and a linear description of the advanced climate-setting competency.

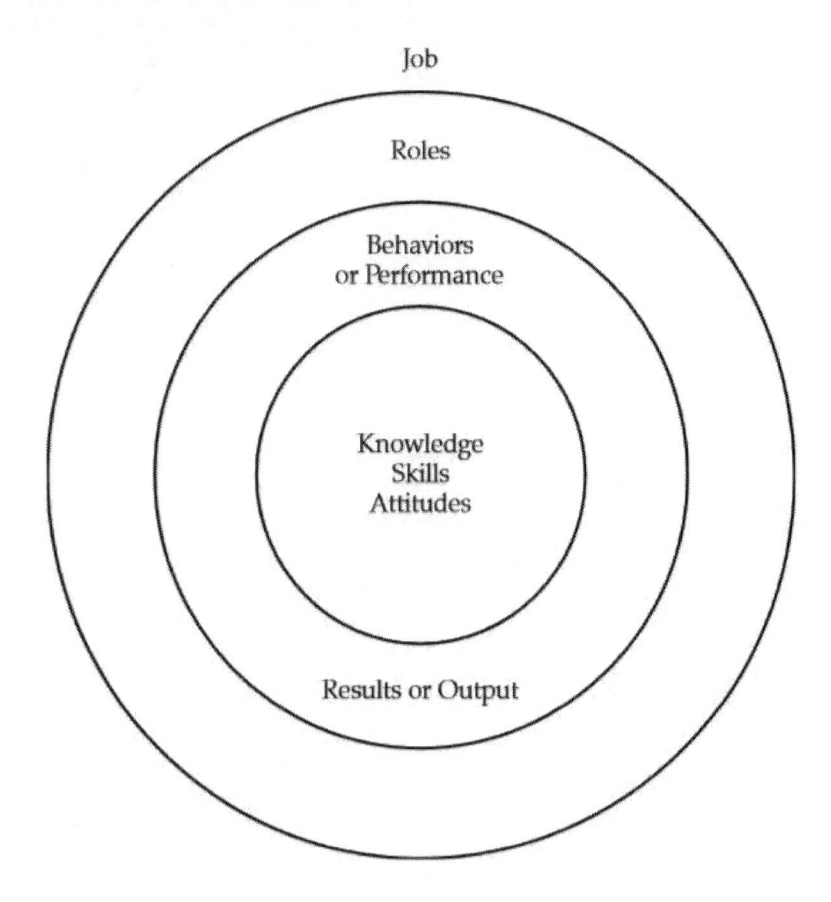

Figure 3.3 The Competency Model

How Competencies Are Measured

Being competent or not is a "pass-fail" measurement. One is either competent or one is not. Either the trainer sets an adult learning climate by being prepared, conducting introductions, and collecting learning objectives, or one of these three elements is missing and therefore the competency is not present. There is no such thing as being 70 percent competent. However, you can be competent 70 percent of the time. There is more than one way to pass or fail. Here is an example of a rating scale to decide whether the competency is present:

A = meets <u>advanced</u> competency (advanced tangible results or output is visible)

B = meets <u>basic</u> competency (tangible results or output is visible)

I = <u>incomplete</u> (tangible results or output is not observed, missing, or partially complete)

N = behavior <u>not</u> observed (not competent)

Notice that it is possible to demonstrate different levels of a single competency. There can be different levels of performance among the competent. Both basic and advanced competencies are described in the list. You can use competency checklists for self-assessment or to give develop- mental feedback to a peer or subordinate. When used in this way, it is important that the rater and the person being observed share a definition of the competencies shown on the checklist. For example, using the list of advanced competencies that follows, a trainer's idea of what constitutes "low risk" for a climate-setting activity may be different from the ideas of the per- son observing that trainer. Prior to rating another person using a competency checklist, review the expanded descriptions with supporting knowledge, skills, and attitudes and ensure that you share a definition of each competency.

Suggested Uses for Competency Checklists

If your organization wishes to create an internal competency and/or certification process, begin involving management, employees, and interested groups to discuss the objectives of this type of assessment process. When rating employees represented by a collective bargaining unit.

Review an individual employee's job description to understand this per- son's role in the training function. Often competencies from more than one role are combined into a single employee's job. Gain agreement between the rater and the person being rated about whether basic or advanced competencies are to be measured.

Use the assessments to develop individual development plans for each staff member. From a composite assessment, identify common developmental needs and make plans to address them. Following the development of these competencies, it may be appropriate to ask training staff to demonstrate their competency in order to take the next step toward certification.

Steps to Set Up a Competency Measurement Process

1. Involve interested managers, employees, and others to agree on the objectives for a competency assessment process in your organization. Decide policy issues such as whether the process will be voluntary or mandatory, which roles will be assessed, what resources will be available for development—identified through the process and time frames. Align this process with other human resource processes such as performance appraisals and compensation and benefits programs.
2. Create a custom assessment checklist for each role that are appropriate to a specific person's job. Add additional competencies as needed.
3. Prior to using the custom competency checklist, the rater and the person being rated should meet and agree on the common meaning of each dimension being measured.

4. Identify when and how the competencies will be observed and rated.
5. Following the observation and rating, the rater and rated person should meet to discuss the ratings. Refer to basic and advanced competency checklists for competencies rated "I" for incomplete or "N" for not observed. Discuss specific knowledge, skills, and attitudes the rater expected to see that were missing.
6. Create a development plan and agree on what resources can be com- mitted to fulfilling the plan. Agree on when the development plan will be completed.

Chapter 6: Trainer or Instructor Competencies

Competencies Required of Trainers or Instructors

Trainers or instructors present information and direct structured learning experiences so individuals increase their knowledge or skills. They also facilitate learning and develop others by using coaching techniques. They prepare for instruction by reviewing course material and making minor adjustments to fit the expected target population. Trainers can use a variety of delivery modes, from one-on-one training and performance coaching to a physical classroom or distance learning in a virtual classroom. The skilled trainer is comfortable using a variety of training methods. Trainers can act as facilitators at staff meetings, at management retreats, or in other situations that require facilitation skills. Trainers also have responsibilities outside the classroom, such as promoting the transfer of learning to the job and making recommendations to course designers regarding course modifications. A variety of titles for trainers or instructors include some of these emerging titles: facilitator, knowledge specialist, learning specialist, online learning specialist, coach, learning coach, and performance improvement specialist.

Competency Checklists for the Trainer or Instructor

Following checklist that lists and defines broad strategic and operational competencies for the trainer or instructor. All the competencies together describe the optimum behaviors for the trainer. When reviewing competencies for a trainer, assess whether the trainer does the tasks described. Ratings of "A" and "B" distinguish whether the competency is held at the "advanced" or "basic" level. For either an "A" or "B" rating, tangible results or outputs are visible. A rating of "I" stands for "incomplete" because tangible results or outputs are not observed, are missing, or are partially complete. Remember that competency is either observed or is not observed.

How to Use the Competency Checklists

Use competency checklists to rate yourself or as part of a collaborative process when being rated by another person. Either eliminate the competencies that do not apply or rate the competency as N/A for "not applicable." Prior to assessing a competency, agree with the rater on the meaning of the competencies. Review the expanded descriptions with supporting knowledge, skills, and attitudes to determine basic versus advanced levels of competency. Also, when rating another person, ensure a shared definition of each competency and what level of competency is being assessed.

Competency Model Checklist for Trainers or Instructors

A = meets advanced competency (advanced tangible results or outputs are visible)
B = meets basic competency (tangible results or outputs are visible)
I = incomplete (tangible results or outputs are not observed, missing or partially complete)
N = behavior not observed (not competent)

Rating	Trainer or Instructor Competency	Basic Results or Output	Advanced Results or Output
	1. Prepares for instruction	Training course announcement Pre-work assignments Room set-up diagram Training equipment materials	Management partnership training course announcement Pre-work assignments Room set-up diagram Training equipment materials
	2. Sets a learning environment	Active participants, completed introductions, posted participant learning objectives.	Active participants, completed introductions music, course graphic, name tents, materials, ground rules are set, objectives posted
	3. Uses adult learning principles	Active participants	Active participants, different

			training methods to appeal to different learning styles.
	4. Uses lecture	Lecture notes, handout materials, visuals	Large group participation, answers participant questions, models platform techniques
	5. Conducts discussions	Agenda, questions summary of ideas	Agenda, questions, summary of ideas, group participation
	6. Facilitates activities	Participants complete activities	Participants complete advanced activities, such as case studies, games, and simulations
	7. Conducts demonstrations	Completed product or completed process	Completed product or completed process, skill performance checklist
	8. Uses role play	Role-play observer's critique sheet, skill development	Role-play observer's critique sheet, empathy or skill development
	9. Gives feedback to learners	Negative feedback, learner changes behavior and learner improves	Positive and negative feedback, learner changes behavior and learner improves
	10. Uses audiovisuals	Equipment and media	Equipment and media that sup-

		identical to handout materials	port handout materials
	11. Administers tests and evaluates skill performance	Scored tests and completed skill performance checklists	Scored tests and completed skill performance checklists timely feedback of test results
	12. Handles problem learners	Problem ignored or problem learner excluded from training	Changed learner behavior
	13. Manages appropriate use of technology	Use of technology	Use of technology
	14. Promotes learning transfer	Transferred learning is used on the job	Transferred learning is used on the job
	15. Conducts learning online	Completed lessons	Completed lessons
	16. Recommends course modifications	Written requests for changes	Written recommendations for changes
	% Total of competencies observed		
	% Total required for competence		

Trainer or Instructor Development Plan Template

Trainer's Name: _____

Date: _____

1. List competencies that exceed expectation:

2. Identify

Underdeveloped or unobserved competencies	Knowledge, skills, and attitudes to acquire

3. Identify competencies that require coaching and feedback:

4. Identify resources required to develop these competencies:

Target date for re-evaluation:

Chapter 7: Training Styles

Trainer Characteristics

Being good at your job does not guarantee that you will be good at training some- one else how to do it. To be effective, trainers must perfect their competencies in the following areas:

- ✓ Training professionals must have a business orientation. They must concern themselves with improving performance and focus on business outcomes.
- ✓ Training professionals must also be able to recognize and admit when training is not the appropriate solution for a problem.
- ✓ To succeed in a diverse environment, trainers must fine-tune their interpersonal skills and be able to adapt to a variety of people, cultures, and situations.
- ✓ Those responsible for training others in a workshop setting must develop and master training skills. True professionals spend their entire lives honing their craft and perfecting their skills, learning new skills, and they keep up- to-date on the latest trends, concepts, and application to the field.

Even if you have never done any formal training or teaching, you have already developed a training style, a combination of training philosophies, methods, and behaviors, as the result of the experiences you have had as a learner and as an unofficial trainer. The way in which you give directions to others (co-workers, friends, family members), present information, or explain how to do something reflects a preferred training style.

Just as you have a preferred style of learning, you have a preferred approach to presenting content and relating to participants. Although you may have a strong preference for one style over another, you can and should learn to use the entire range of styles to connect with participants and facilitate the learning process. Much like management or leadership styles, inherent in training styles is the need to balance continually concern for task or content with concern for people. This is further complicated by the fact that different training styles impact different types of learners in different ways.

To heighten your awareness of your own style preferences, complete the assessment instrument in figure 3.4 using your most recent training assignment as a frame of reference. You are evaluating yourself as "the trainer" and thus ranking statements in terms of how you think you behave. To gain a more accurate and complete picture of your training style, ask others to evaluate you by completing the assessment, and then compare results.

Figure 3.4 Instructional Styles Diagnosis Inventory

Instructions: Think of your most recent learning experience with the trainer who is being evaluated. Each of the twenty items that follows contains four statements about what instructors can do or ways in which they can act. Rank each set of statements to reflect the degree to which each statement in the set describes the trainer's instructional style. Assign a ranking of four (4) to the statement most characteristic or descriptive of the trainer; assign a three (3) to the next most descriptive statement; a two (2) to the next most descriptive statement; and a one (1) to the statement that is least descriptive of the trainer. Record your response for each statement in the blank next to it. For some items, you may think that all statements are very descriptive or that none fit very well. To give the most accurate feedback, force yourself to rank the statements as best you can.

"When Instructing Adults, This Person Would Be Most Likely to..."

1.
_____ a. Allow extended practice or discussion in areas of particular interest to learners.
_____ b. Judge trainer's effectiveness by how well the prepared materials are covered.
_____ c. Sit down with learners while instructing them.
_____ d. Set trainer up as a role model and encourage learners to emulate trainer.

2.
_____ a. End a training session by summarizing the key subject matter and recommending that learners find ways to apply it on the job.
_____ b. Arrange the room so as to provide for better discipline and control.
_____ c. Use specific course objectives to inform learners as to what they should expect to be able to do.
_____ d. Focus learners' attention more on themselves and their own performance than on trainer.

3.
_____ a. Gain supervisors' involvement by providing ideas on how to support learners' attempts to apply new skills.
_____ b. Let the group "handle" difficult learners or privately explore reasons for problems.
_____ c. Evaluate learners by giving examinations to test their retention of presented materials.
_____ d. Carefully lead and control any group discussions.

4.
_____ a. Put his or her primary focus on giving a technically polished presentation.
_____ b. Avoid reducing impact by not disclosing any course materials prior to the program.
_____ c. Show willingness to learn from learners by admitting errors or lack of knowledge when appropriate.

____ d. Collect background information and adjust the level of content material for each particular group.

5.
____ a. Involve learners in activities designed to stimulate critical or reflective thought.
____ b. Communicate positive expectations to slower learners through feed- back and encouragement, in order to help them improve.
____ c. Motivate learners with enthusiastic talks, humorous stories, and entertaining or inspirational videos.
____ d. Maintain punctuality of published program schedules.

6.
____ a. Make occasional use of media tools to support other primary learning activities.
____ b. Present materials in the most logical order.
____ c. Allow learners to influence or prioritize course content and objectives.
____ d. Ensure that learners perform and apply newly learned skills as instructed.

7.
____ a. Thoroughly cover all subject-matter areas in the scheduled time allotted.
____ b. Change course materials or training methods based on feedback about performance changes after training.
____ c. Maintain a consistent pace of presentation throughout the program.
____ d. Express concern for and interest in individual learners and their problems.

8.
____ a. Judge trainer's effectiveness based on learners' "lik-

ing" of trainer.
_____ b. Allow learners to make mistakes and learn from session experiences.
_____ c. Expose learners to traditionally accepted subject matter and correct procedures.
_____ d. Ask learners questions designed to guide them to self-discovery of key points.

9.
_____ a. Frequently assess learners' body language and emotional states and adjust activities or schedule appropriately.
_____ b. Explore content-related controversial issues as potential learning experiences.
_____ c. Plan and structure course materials in considerable detail.
_____ d. Begin program by informing learners of trainer's experience or qualifications and trainer's goals for the program.

10.
_____ a. Cite a bibliography of resources concerning materials discussed for further learner self-development.
_____ b. Use position as instructor to quickly resolve "difficult learner" problems (e.g., monopolizes, side conversations, sharpshooters, etc.).
_____ c. Encourage casual or comfortable dress to increase the informality of the learning environment.
_____ d. Avoid potentially time-wasting tangents by dealing with learners' questions quickly and moving on.

11.
_____ a. Direct learners' attention primarily to trainer and to what is being said or demonstrated.
_____ b. Frequently redirect learners' questions to other learners to be answered.
_____ c. Send out self-study "pre-work" materials to spark learner interest and formation of course expectations.

       ____ d. Consistently cover the same material with each group.

12.
       ____ a. Arrange the room so as to promote group activities and discussions.
       ____ b. Always stand in front of the class while instructing.
       ____ c. Send learners' bosses an overview of course subject matter.
       ____ d. Judge trainer's effectiveness based on how proficient learners are in performing new skills or applying new concepts on the job.

13.
       ____ a. Project a professional image by maintaining a separation between trainer and learners.
       ____ b. Help learners motivate themselves by developing new skills through involvement and participation.
       ____ c. Closely direct learners' activities.
       ____ d. Allow learners to analyze materials and draw their own conclusions.

14.
       ____ a. End a training session by helping learners create action plans to apply course content to real-world problems.
       ____ b. Criticize slow learners to help them improve.
       ____ c. Avoid controversy as a potential distraction or turnoff.
       ____ d. Coach learners as they practice new skills.

15.
       ____ a. Encourage detailed note taking by learners
       ____ b. Encourage learners to challenge outdated course materials or concepts of questionable value on the job.

_____ c. Sequence activities so as to stimulate and hold learner interest.
_____ d. Use media (video, slides, overheads, etc.) extensively to increase the professionalism of the presentation.

16.
_____ a. Use an introductory overview to inform learners of the subject matter to be covered.
_____ b. Judge trainer's effectiveness based on learners' increase in confidence and self-esteem.
_____ c. Maintain a formal dress code to establish a more serious atmosphere.
_____ d. Encourage creativity in the performance and application of course concepts.

17.
_____ a. Change course materials or training methods based on update of expertise in the subject matter.
_____ b. Begin a program by having learners introduce themselves to one another and communicate to trainer what their expectations are.
_____ c. Adjust time schedules during the program in response to learners' interests and concerns.
_____ d. Enhance credibility with learners by answering all questions quickly and accurately.

18.
_____ a. Avoid potentially embarrassing questions and protect material by keeping content resources confidential.
_____ b. Highlight key points in detail, speaking from carefully prepared notes.
_____ c. Vary pace of the program to adjust to natural daily highs and lows in learners' energy levels.
_____ d. Evaluate learners based on their abilities to perform specific objectives.

19.
_____ a. Defend trainer's expertise and credibility when challenged by a learner on a content issue.

    ____   b. Emphasize establishing open, two-way communication.

    ____   c. Leave the structure of the program loose to respond to the specific needs of the group.

    ____   d. Aim the level of sophistication of course material at the "average" learner.

20.

    ____   a. Listen attentively and observe group discussion of content issues or problem applications.

    ____   b. Ensure that learners reach the right conclusions and accept the key points or concepts presented.

    ____   c. Explore reasons that learners ask questions, to bring out individual concerns and hidden agendas.

    ____   d. Project confidence and assurance by using effective gestures, posture, and vocal dynamics while instructing.

Instructional styles diagnosis inventory scoring sheet
(To be completed by trainer)

Step 1 Instructions: Transfer the rankings from the ISDI to the Scoring Chart below. Note that the letter items in each set are not in alphabetical order.

Scoring Chart				
	A	**B**	**C**	**D**
1	d	a	c	b
2	b	c	d	a
3	d	a	b	c
4	a	b	c	d
5	c	a	b	d
6	b	c	a	d
7	c	b	d	a
8	a	b	d	c
9	d	b	a	c
10	b	a	d	c
11	a	c	b	d
12	b	d	a	c
13	a	d	b	c
14	b	a	d	c
15	d	b	c	a
16	c	d	b	a
17	d	c	b	a
18	b	d	c	a
19	a	c	b	d
20	d	c	a	b
Total	___	___	___	___

Step 2 Determine the sum of the rankings in each column and record them at the bottom of that column.

Step 3 Subtract the lower of the Column A or C totals from the higher.

Step 4 Subtract the lower of the Column B and D totals from the higher.

Step 5 Plot the result from Step 3 on the vertical scale of the graph that follows. If the "A" total is higher, plot the result below the midpoint "O." If the "C" total is higher, plot the result above this point.

Step 6 Plot the result from Step 4 on the horizontal scale. If the "B" total is higher, plot the result to the right of the midpoint "O." If the "D" total is higher, plot the result to the left of this point.

Step 7 Extend lines from the plotted points on each scale to the point where the two lines intersect.

```
                                    60
                                    50   I                              IV
                                    40
                         LEARNERS   30        SELLER         COACH
                                    20
                                    10
                WHO?                 0 ─────────────────────────────────
                                    10
                         INSTRUCTOR 20
                                    30       PROFESSOR    ENTERTAINER
                                    40
                                    50   II                             III
                                    60
                                        60 50 40 30 20 10  0 10 20 30 40 50 60

                                        ←──── CONTENT ──────── LEARNING ────→
                                                    WHAT?
```

Descriptions of Styles

Following are short descriptions of the types of behaviors, attitudes, tendencies, and preferences that characterize each of the four styles.

The Seller

A person who has the "seller" instructional style is primarily concerned with the content and how positively it is received and understood. Learning is the participant's responsibility, and it may or may not happen as a result. Because getting the message across and creating a good attitude toward it are the primary goals, "seller" instructors tend to focus their attention on the learners and the learners' receptivity to the message.

They build a receptive atmosphere by creating a comfortable learning environment, encouraging learners, answering questions, varying the pace of the program, and so on. They tend to use lectures or prepared media presentation methods, interspersed with discussion to hold interest and attention. Note taking is encouraged to aid retention of material.

Homework, pre-work, and course-summary materials are used extensively to communicate or reinforce the content. Pass/fail or no graded examinations are preferred to assess retention without turning the learners off.

The "seller" style is common in public schools and is probably more appropriate for building general educational backgrounds than for developing specific skills. It may also be appropriate for situations in which the selling of a technique, concept, or product is more important than the learners' becoming proficient in it. It is not as appropriate when learners are expected to perform better or differently as a result of the training.

The Professor

Instructors who have a high concern for both content and delivery probably see themselves primarily as presenters. The "professor" types tend to be highly concerned about such things as their image, their technique and smoothness of speaking, and creating a proper impression. They prefer to have the spotlight on themselves, because this focuses the learners' attention on them. The atmosphere in their sessions tends to be formal, and the separation between the presenter and the audience is emphasized.

"Professor" types are, at the same time, concerned with the adequacy of what they are presenting. Their presentations are usually well-researched, often impressively footnoted and referenced, planned and organized in detail, and well- rehearsed. Time is important because it reflects on their images as presenters (i.e., punctuality is impressive) and on their ability to cover all important content. Their preferred teaching method is to lecture, as this allows them to focus attention on themselves, to control time, and to cover the content they believe is important. There is a tendency to overuse or inappropriately use media such as video, slides, or overheads because of their perceived ability to impress, entertain, and present large amounts of information in short time spans.

Typical situations where the "professor" style would be appropriate are making a speech, delivering an after-dinner talk, communicating a report, and presenting or selling ideas to decision makers. This style usually is not as effective where actual skill development or behavioral change is expected from the learners. It may be appropriate for attitude change purposes; however, change produced by this method typically is short-lived unless constantly reinforced.

The Entertainer

Instructors who use the "entertainer" style focus on the results of training but also feel that people will learn best from instructors they like, respect, or admire. They have many of the same personal-image concerns as "professors." They are very concerned with their credibility and whether the learners have confidence in their expertise. "Entertainers" are concerned about involvement in the learning process, but more with their own than with the learners'. Thus, methods such as watching a role model (the instructor) demonstrate proper technique are preferred over self- discovery or group learning activities. When more participatory methods are used, these instructors tend to exercise close control and make themselves an integral part of the learning process. Because these instructors generally believe that learners need to be "inspired" if they are going to perform differently, sessions often are designed to be highly motivational or entertaining. This can be effective but has the potential limitation of making what is learned instructor-dependent. When this occurs, learners can suffer drops in motivation when attempting to apply new skills on the job because the dynamic instructor is not there. The fact that they are personally influencing learners is often more important to these instructors than the specific change that takes place or the input that causes it. Thus, specific content is not an important issue. This style probably is most appropriate for personal growth seminars, sales meetings, and programs that are meant to "recharge learners' batteries." In its worst case, the "entertainer" style could be likened to a medicine-show huckster who dazzles you and takes your money before you have a chance to judge the value of his product.

The Coach

Instructors who are oriented both to learning and to the learners tend to have the spotlight reversed so that the learners' attention is focused on themselves most of the time. These trainers see their role more as facilitators of learning experiences than as presenters of information. They see value in course content only insofar as it enables learners to perform in new ways. The focus of most coaching activities is on skill development, confidence building, and application, rather than on retention of information. Learners are evaluated, but mostly through observation of performance or behavioral change rather than through written tests. Grades usually are ignored, because most instruction is aimed at upgrading everyone's skills to a minimum or improved level rather than on determining who is most proficient. There is less concern for polished delivery because "coach" instructors spend much less time "delivering." Also, because of the informal atmosphere created, there is less pressure on the instructor to perform, motivate, or entertain. Use of a high ratio of self-discovery and group-learning activities allows the learners to motivate and entertain themselves. The responsibility to perform is, in effect, shifted from the instructor to them. Separation between the instructor and the learners is de-emphasized. The prevailing philosophy typically is that the best instructor is the one who sets high expectations, guides and coaches the learners, and then gets out of the way so they can perform. The instructor has a message, but the message is determined more by specific learner needs and less by what the instructor thinks might be good for the learners. Rather than forcing learners to understand and accept new ideas, "coaches" use questions, discussions, self-study, group work, and other involving techniques to lead learners to conclusions, but they allow the learners to make the commitments on their own. The "coach" style tends to be most effective in bona fide training situations where skill building and behavioral change are the primary concerns. Potential problems with this style are tendencies to ignore time constraints, skip over important content issues, lose control of the class, turn off learners who are used to more traditional instructional styles, or be overly influenced by learners' perceptions of their own needs.

ISDI QUICK REFERENCE GUIDE

WHO? ← LEARNERS / INSTRUCTOR →
CONTENT ← → LEARNING

SELLER	COACH
Sellers are: Task-oriented	Coaches are: Learner-oriented
They see themselves as: Taskmasters/persuaders	They see themselves as: Facilitators/guides
Sellers' main concern is: Product/content	Coaches' main concern is: Results/performance
They strive to be: Driving, aggressive, enthusiastic, convincing	They strive to be: Driving, accepting, empathic, supportive
Programs are structured to be: Informal but inflexible	Programs are structured to be: Informal and flexible
Leading to sessions that are: Informative, productive, efficient, complete, persuasive	Leading to sessions that are: Involving, encouraging, constructive, developmental
Learners are evaluated by: Objective testing	Learners are evaluated by: Comparing behaviors or performance objectives

PROFESSOR	ENTERTAINER
Professors are: Instructor-oriented	Entertainers are: Relations-oriented
They see themselves as: Presenters/experts	They see themselves as: Role models/stars
Sellers' main concern is: Process/delivery	Entertainers' main concern is: Reactions/feelings
They strive to be: Impressive, polished, professional, aloof	They strive to be: Dynamic, animated, charismatic, outgoing, inspirational
Programs are structured to be: Formal and inflexible	Programs are structured to be: Formal but flexible
Leading to sessions that are: Scheduled, controlled, organized, disciplined	Leading to sessions that are: Motivated, lively, fun, entertaining
Learners are evaluated by: Subjective testing and instructor judgement	Learners are evaluated by: Assessment of their feelings and opinions

Chapter 8: Understanding Adult Learner

Although adult education theorists differ on just how different adults are from children, most embrace the andragogical theory of adult learning. During the 1960s, European adult educators coined the term "andragogy" to provide a label for a growing body of knowledge and technology in regard to adult learning. The concept was introduced and advanced in the United States by Malcolm Knowles. The following assumptions underlie the andragogical model of learning, which Knowles now calls a model of human learning (Knowles, 1990):

Assumption One:

The first assumption involves a change in self-concept from total dependency to in- creasing self-directedness. The adult learner is self-directed. Adult learners want to take responsibility for their own lives, including the planning, implementing, and evaluating of their learning activities. This principle is often misinterpreted. Learner self-directedness does not mean the trainer abdicates responsibility for the plan or approach. From the beginning, the trainer establishes the training process as a collaborative effort. Throughout the process, the trainer and participant should be partners engaged in ongoing, two-way communication.

Assumption Two:

The second principle addresses the role of experience, a principle unique to the adult learner. According to Knowles, each of us brings to a learning situation a wealth of experiences that provide a base for new learning as well as a resource to share with others. These experiences may be good or bad, but they will impact the way in which an employee approaches a new learning experience. Because people base their learning on past experiences, the new information must be assimilated. The wise trainer will find out what the participants already know and will build on those experiences, rather than treating participants as though they know nothing and must be taught like small children.

Assumption Three:

The third assumption is that adults are ready to learn when they perceive a need to know or do something in order to perform more effectively in some aspect of their lives. The days of abstract theories and concepts are over for most adults. They want the learning experience to be practical and realistic, problem-centered rather than subject-centered. The effective trainer helps participants understand how learning a particular skill or task will help them be more successful, that is, how the employee can do the job quicker, easier, more efficiently.

Assumption Four:

Fourth, adults want immediate, real-world applications. They want the skills and knowledge to help them solve problems or complete tasks. People are motivated to learn when they see relevance to their real-life situations and are able to apply what they have learned as quickly as possible. Therefore, learning activities need to be clearly relevant to the immediate needs of the adult. To be effective, deliver just-in-time training and emphasize how the training is going to make participants' jobs easier.

Assumption Five:

Finally, adults are motivated to learn because of internal factors such as self-esteem, desire for recognition, natural curiosity, innate love of learning, better quality of life, greater self-confidence, or the opportunity to self-actualize.

As you begin to design and develop any training program for adults, keep in mind these additional principles regarding how adults learn:

- Adults prefer the concrete to the abstract.
- Adults need a variety of training methods.
- Adults learn better in an informal, comfortable environment.
- Adults want to solve realistic problems.
- Adults prefer the hands-on method of learning.

Adults learn through a variety of ways. One person may learn better by listening; another may be visual or may prefer to read instructions. Someone else will need a demonstration. Learning style refers to the way in which a learner approaches and responds to a learning experience.

To get a flavor for these style differences and to further your understanding of your preferred learning style, complete the learning style assessment, then score and study it.

1. When solving a problem, I prefer to. . .
    a. take a step-by-step approach
    b. take immediate action
    c. consider the impact on others
    d. make sure I have all the facts

2. As a learner, I prefer to. . .
    a. listen to a lecture
    b. work in small groups
    c. read articles and case studies
    d. participate in role plays

3. When the trainer asks a question to which I know the answer, I. . .
    a. let others answer first
    b. offer an immediate response
    c. consider whether my answer will be received favorably
    d. think carefully about my answer before responding

4. In a group discussion, I. . .
    a. encourage others to offer their opinions
    b. question others' opinions

     c. readily offer my opinion
     d. listen to others before offering my opinion

5. I learn best from activities in which I. . .
    a. can interact with others
    b. remain uninvolved
    c. take a leadership role
    d. can take my time

6. During a lecture, I listen for. . .
    a. practical how-to's
    b. logical points
    c. the main idea
    d. stories and anecdotes

7. I am impressed by a trainer's. . .
    a. knowledge and expertise
    b. personality and style
    c. use of methods and activities
    d. organization and control

8. I prefer information to be presented in the following way:
    a. a model such as a flow chart
    b. bullet points
    c. detailed explanation
    d. accompanied by examples

9. I learn best when I. . .
    a. see relationships among ideas, events, and situations
    b. interact with others
    c. receive practical tips
    d. observe a demonstration or video

10. Before attending a training program, I ask myself: "Will I. . .?"
    a. get practical tips to help me in my job
    b. receive lots of information
    c. have to participate
    d. learn something new

11. After attending a training session, I...
    a. tend to think about what I learned
    b. am anxious to put my learning into action
    c. reflect on the experience as a whole
    d. tell others about my experience

12. The training method I dislike the most is...
    a. participating in small groups
    b. listening to a lecture
    c. reading and analyzing case studies
    d. participating in role plays

Scoring Sheet

Instructions: Record your responses on the appropriate spaces below, then total the columns.

Feeler	Observer	Thinker	Doer
1c___	1a___	1d___	1b___
2b___	2a___	2c___	2d___
3c___	3a___	3d___	3b___
4a___	4d___	4b___	4c___
5a___	5b___	5d___	5c___
6d___	6c___	6b___	6a___
7b___	7d___	7a___	7c___
8a___	8d___	8c___	8b___
9b___	9d___	9a___	9c___
10d___	10c___	10b___	10a___
11d___	11c___	11a___	11b___
12c___	12a___	12d___	12b___

Feelers are very people-oriented. They are expressive and focus on feelings and emotions. They enjoy affective learning and gravitate toward learning experiences that explore people's attitudes and emotions. Feelers thrive in an open, unstructured learning environment and appreciate the opportunity to work in groups and like activities in which they can share opinions and experiences.

Observers like to watch and listen. They tend to be reserved and quiet and will take their time before acting or participating in class. When they do decide to offer an opinion or answer a question, they are generally right on target. They enjoy learning experiences that allow them to consider various ideas and opinions, and they seem to thrive on learning through discovery.

Thinkers rely on logic and reason. They like the opportunity to share ideas and concepts. They prefer activities that require them to analyze and evaluate. They will question the rationale behind activities and will challenge statements that they perceive to be too general or without substance. The thinkers prefer to work independently and question the relevance of role plays and simulations.

Doers like to be actively involved in the learning process. They will take charge in group activities and tend to dominate discussions. They like opportunities to practice what they learned, and they are particularly interested in knowing how they are going to apply what they learn in the real world. They like information presented clearly and concisely and become impatient with drawn-out discussions.

Keep in mind that no one learning style is right or even better than another. The point is that each person learns differently. A variety of learning styles will be rep- resented in any training session. To be effective, trainers must design their pro- grams to accommodate style differences. Predictably, trainers use the styles they prefer. Although it is natural to use the style with which one is most comfortable, the most effective trainers will learn how to adapt their styles to meet the needs of all participants.

In addition to learning styles, an effective trainer must be able to understand the different perceptual modalities. According to M.B. James and M.W. Galbraith (1985), a learner may prefer one of the following six perceptual modalities, ways in which one takes in and processes information:

Visual   Videos; slides; graphs; photos; demonstrations; meth-

	ods and media that create opportunities for the participant to experience learning through the eyes.
Print	Texts; paper-and-pencil exercises that enable the participant to absorb the written word.
Aural	Lectures; audiotapes; methods that allow the participant to simply listen and take in information through the ears.
Interactive	Group discussions; question-and-answer sessions; ways that give the participant an opportunity to talk and engage in an exchange of ideas, opinions, reactions with fellow participants.
Tactile	Hands-on activities; model building methods that require the participant to handle objects or put things together.
Kinesthetic	Role plays; physical games and activities that involve the use of psychomotor skills and movement from one place to another

Our minds are like sponges as we soak up knowledge and information. When sponges are saturated, any additional water will run right through. Just as the sponge is overloaded, a learner can experience cognitive overload of his or her working memory. This working memory—the center of conscious thinking—has an estimated limited capacity of seven "chunks" or pieces of information. The limits on our working memory depend on the knowledge we have stored in long-term memory. A person who is quite comfortable with and knowledgeable about a subject can easily overwhelm those who are less familiar with the information. The challenge to the trainer is to present information in such a way that the participants do not experience overload.

To prevent cognitive overload, use the following strategies when designing, developing, and delivering your training:

- Minimize the use of lecture.
- Have the participants do most of the work.
- Create chunks of content or information, and distribute or communicate it incrementally.

- Design workbooks and other participant materials that present information in an easy-to-follow and easy-to-understand format.
- Create job aids for use during and after the training.

These concepts have certain implications for the trainer. The traditional or pedagogical orientation is concerned with content. Trainers are concerned with "covering" material in the most efficient way possible. In contrast, the andragogical orientation focuses on process, being attentive to the factors that either promote or inhibit learning.

Chapter 9: Analyses for Training

Ideally, the decision to use training to overcome an actual shortfall in performance or to prevent a shortfall occurring in the future, should have been taken after the trainer and the client have studied the results of some form of reactive or proactive investigation. The trainer is then able to address the basic and critical issues:

- What should be the specific content of the training?
- How should the training be organized and implemented?
- How, in terms of effectiveness, should the training be evaluated?

Davies (1971) argues that high costs may be incurred as a result of too much training because:

- More training is being organized than is really necessary.
- Courses and training programs are longer than they need to be.
- More instructors/tutors and equipment are employed than the job demands.
- Students, who may be perfectly competent in performing the job, fail the training because it is too theoretical rather than practical in its nature.
- Irrelevant criteria may be used to select students for training resulting in potentially suitable students being excluded from the program.
- Job dissatisfaction can result from the worker being prepared for a higher caliber job than the one being done. In turn this could lead to higher turnover of personnel, poorer performance, etc.

Naturally, because of the time and expense involved, the trainer must give very careful thought to the scope and depth of any further analyses. In considering the question of scope, Kenny and Reid (1986) suggest three approaches that are particularly appropriate to organization training: comprehensive analysis, key-task analysis and problem centered analysis.

Comprehensive analysis

In this approach all aspects of the job are scrutinized. The intention is to produce a comprehensive and detailed list or record of every task and sub-task that make up the job together with the knowledge, skills and attitudes which are needed to perform the tasks and sub-tasks effectively. As this approach is very likely to be costly and time-consuming, certain criteria should be satisfied before the trainer undertakes such a study. Kenny and Reid suggest the following criteria:

- The tasks are unfamiliar to trainees or potential trainees, they are difficult to learn and the costs of failure or error are unacceptable in terms of expenditure of money, time and human effort.
- Resources are available to carry out such analyses.
- The training program that results from this approach will be used frequently and should, therefore, be cost-effective.
- The tasks comprising the job are laid down in a tight and closely prescribed manner and the right way of carrying them out must be learned and adhered to.
- Management understands and accept the need for this type of approach to be adopted

The circumstances or situations that are likely to warrant this level and extent of analysis are:

- The introduction of new equipment, technology or procedures that necessitate either the creation of entirely different jobs or the acquisition of an extensive range of new skills, etc.
- Thorough update of training in a particular functional area where current training has been allowed to 'drift' and general performance has become poor.
- Creation of a new position as a result of changing market conditions.
- The introduction of planned training into a functional area where no formal training has existed previously but changing technical requirements and developments make it imperative for the manpower concerned to be 're-fitted' and updated.

Key-task analysis

This form of analysis is concerned mainly with the identification and detailed investigation of key or primary tasks within the job. It has particular relevance to managerial and supervisory positions that consist of many tasks of which not all are critical for effective performance. It is also relevant to jobs that change in emphasis or content leading to a need to establish priority tasks and to identify the knowledge and skills which are required and to establish an acceptable standard of performance. Kenny and Reid reinforce the point that a fully comprehensive analysis of managerial and supervisory jobs would be too expensive and unwieldy to be viable. Key-task analysis would probably result in a job description that only highlights key or critical tasks and an outline of the knowledge, skills and attitudes required to perform the job.

Problem-centered analysis

Attention is focused neither on the whole nor necessarily on all of the critical or key tasks but on those aspects of current performance that are below standard. In cases such as these it will have been decided already that training is an appropriate way to overcome the problem or difficulty which has been identified and that a more extensive analysis is unnecessary because the performance of the job holders is quite satisfactory in other respects.

Beyond the concern about the scope of the investigation, the trainer then has to decide upon the specific analyses that have to be carried out and what associated analytical methods and techniques should be used. Figure 3.5 illustrates diagrammatically the sequence of stages or steps that a trainer may have to follow in order to determine the content of training. The direction of the arrows in the diagram are intended to indicate that the different types of analyses are not mutually exclusive or independent and that data gathered at an early stage may reduce the extent of, or even the necessity for, subsequent analyses. For example, information stemming from the reactive route into training may mean that only a limited job analysis needs to be undertaken. Again, a thorough job analysis which produces a detailed and comprehensive job specification may suggest that any additional analyses can be by-passed. The analyses referred to in Figure 3.5 and the associated analytical techniques and methods can now be looked at in more detail.

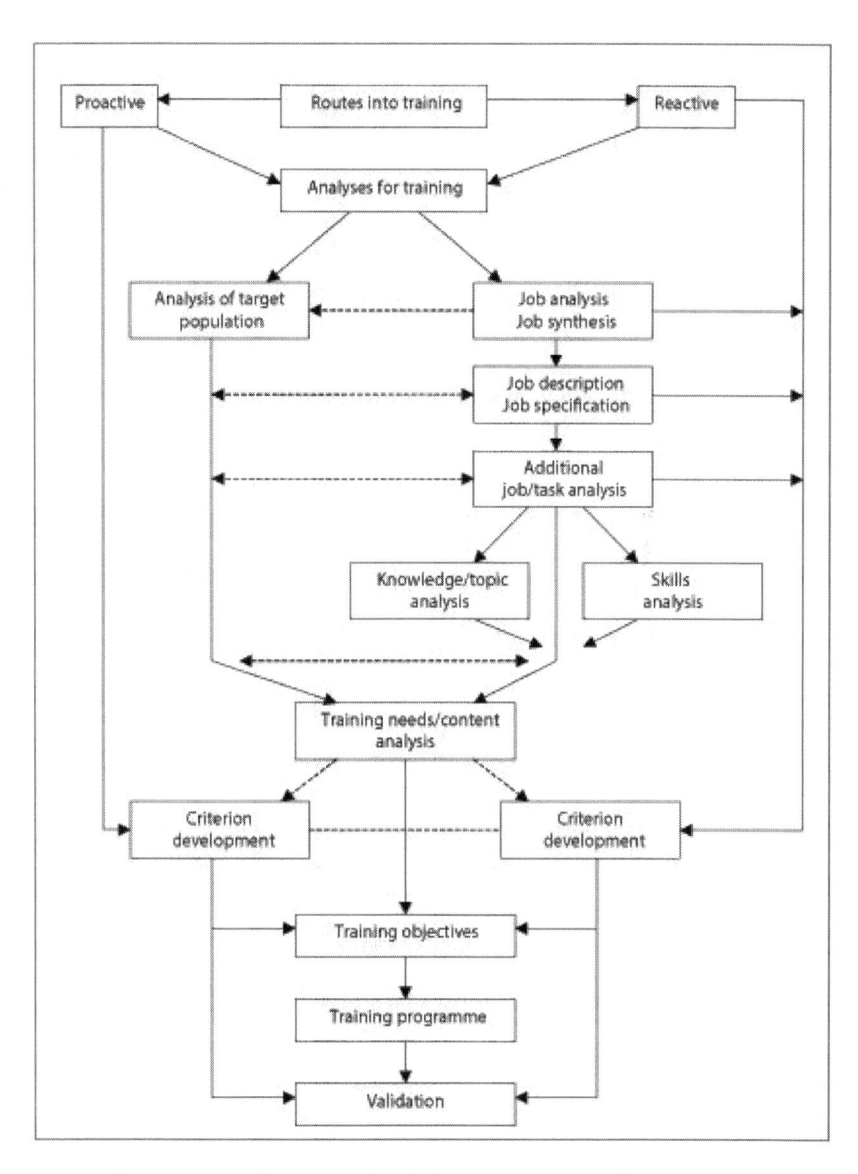

Figure 3.5   Stages/steps leading to training needs/content and beyond

Job analysis

Job analysis can be used for a number of different purposes which include personnel selection, job evaluation and training. The Glossary of Training Terms (Department of Employment, 1978) describes job analysis as:

> The process of examining a job in detail in order to identify its component tasks. The detail and approach may vary according to the purpose for which the job is being analyzed, eg training, equipment design, work layout.

To many, the process of job analysis has associations with time-and-motion studies and may appear to be a lengthy, dull and uninteresting activity. To employees it is often viewed with suspicion, like many other forms of analysis, and they feel that there is a hidden or secret motive which could threaten their livelihood. There are some who use the term 'job analysis' as being synonymous with training-needs analysis and gain the false impression that all analyses of training needs involve lengthy procedures before any hint of training is given. Ideally, a job analysis should only have to be done once in the lifespan of a particular job. Many diagrammatic representations of a systematic approach to training show job analysis as an early stage in the process of training design. All such systems are intended to be self-regulating so that any changes in the job procedures or equipment, etc should be fed into the system so that the information held by the trainers can be updated. In theory this is a sensible and logical process but in practice it is all too rare. The usual outcome of a job analysis is a job description or the more detailed job specification and these should be the documents that a trainer should want to look at first. In many cases, job descriptions are out-of-date, thin on content or non-existent, while some human resource departments review job descriptions annually and indicate that they have been either 'revised' or 'reviewed' on a specific date. When this is the case, the trainer's job becomes easier. When it is necessary to undertake a job analysis, many of the techniques which have been described already may be used, such as the structured interview, observation, questionnaire, etc.

Other forms of analysis which often are used interchangeably with job analysis are task analysis and skills analysis. In essence the trainer has to delve deeper into jobs in order to find out more about the duties or tasks which make up the job description so that suitable training can be designed. The Glossary of Training Terms defines task analysis as:

> A systematic analysis of the behavior required to carry out a task with a view to identifying areas of difficulty and the appropriate training techniques and learning aids necessary for successful instruction.

This definition points much more clearly to the training function than that of the job description. Pearn and Kandola (1988) deliberately avoid the use of the term 'job analyses because of what they see as its self-perpetuating dull and uninteresting image. They prefer to use the term 'job, task and role (JTR) analysis' as a research tool that has many more applications for managers

Job synthesis and future-oriented job analysis

The notion of future-oriented job analysis has been discussed by Hall (1986) in relation to succession planning for executive positions. This process would first of all involve an examination of an organization's corporate objectives and strategies. From this examination the anticipated executive job demands and the necessary skills required by future executives to meet these demands could be derived. As Hall points out, 'Thinking through this link between the organization's basic objectives and need for future top executive skills is the core of strategic succession planning' and must be the basis for identifying the future training and development needs of these individuals.

When a job is new, when it has been changed greatly or when new tasks have been added to it, it is not possible to write a job description or a job specification using the same analytical techniques. It should not be regarded as an appropriate method to throw job holders in at the deep end and wait until they have mastered the job before any analysis begins. The end result could be very costly to the organization. However, that is not to say that some trial and error should not be involved in the way that the job develops. Job synthesis is the technique by which a new job or task can be examined in order to produce a job specification and, subsequently, appropriate training. A number of people are likely to be involved in developing the new job or task and in many cases it would be them to whom the trainer would turn to assist with an analysis. The products or outputs would provide a first indicator of what the job is about; for example, it might be a new piece of machinery, a new technique of food preparation or a new service. It is possible that there are other jobs which are related to the new one, the holders of which can contribute to the structure of the new job or task.

When this is not the case, it may be possible to tap the experience of those in other organizations or to recruit new staff with relevant experience. In organizations which are large enough to have an organization and methods department, much of the trial-and-error work will have been done by them. Where this is the case the trainer should have been involved at an early stage in the development. Subsequently, the involvement of managers and supervisors can contribute through technical conferences and trials with job holders to build up a picture of the knowledge and skills, and the activities or tasks which must be performed to achieve the results required. It is unlikely that the job specification will be perfect at the first attempt and all training developed through job synthesis should be monitored carefully and reviewed frequently. The first products of a job analysis or job synthesis of particular relevance for training are a job description and a job specification.

A job description
This has been defined as a general statement of the purpose, scope, responsibilities and duties which make up a particular job. The layout of a typical job description format, including any explanatory notes, is set out below:

1. *Job title* generally speaking the job title should be succinct and, as far as possible, a realistic reflection of the nature of the job.
2. *Division/Department/Section* This information will help to identify where the job 'fits' in the organization.
3. *Location of job* This refers to where the job holder normally performs the duties, etc which make up the job. If

the job is peripatetic then that feature may be mentioned here.
4. *Main purpose of the job* It may be valuable to have a brief statement of the main purpose or general aim of the job in order to appreciate how it helps to fulfill unit, section, departmental or divisional objectives.
5. *Duties/Responsibilities/Tasks* The duties and responsibilities provide the main headings and sub-divisions of the job. Under these should be listed the specific tasks to be performed.
6. *Responsible* to This should state the position of the job holder's immediate superior and sometimes include the frequency and closeness of supervision. Ungerson (1983) suggests 'this first, apparently simple, piece of recording can give warning of fundamental weaknesses or muddle in the organization'.
7. *Relationships*
8. *Judgment*
9. *Physical working conditions*
10. *Social working conditions*
11. *Economic working conditions*
12. *Prospects and current training/Developments opportunities*
13. *Difficulties/Distastes and satisfactions*
14. *Reasons for failure*

A job specification

This is a detailed statement of the knowledge and the physical and mental activities required to carry out the tasks which constitute the job. A job specification pro forma might have the following headings:

Duty/responsibility and task/task element

A task/task element is a clearly definable activity forming part of a main duty or responsibility.

Knowledge/comprehension

What the person undertaking the task must know or understand in order to carry out the job to an adequate standard and would cover.

Skills/abilities
A series of behaviors or acts that form the task and which require practice in order for the task to be performed satisfactorily. The skill or ability may be psycho-motor (manual), social/interpersonal or intellectual.

Attitudes
In this context attitudes refers to the feelings or emotional reaction towards or against something or someone, which may affect job behavior in a positive or negative way.

	Job description	Task/Task element	Knowledge	Skill	Attitude
Title:	Representative	1. To plan work			
Department:	Sales	1.1 To make cycle plan	Square number and company breakdown of area; location and availability of customers; customer records; location of potential customers; market days and early closing days; sales targets and budgets	Time estimation Map reading Record keeping	Must value the relationship between planned (efficient) activity and profitability
Function:	To increase the profitable sales of company products to potential customers in the area				
Reports to:	Field Sales Executive				

Duties and responsibilities:

1. To plan work
2. To make sales to…
3. To send in orders
4. To seek new business/customers
5. To assess competitor activity
6. To carry out various analytical tests
7. To liaise with company personnel
8. To assist with deliveries
9. To deal with certain financial matters
10. To deal with complaints and queries
11. To attend various meetings and courses
12. To keep abreast of all developments and up-to-date

	1.2 To use telephone to sell, and to book and cancel appointments	Telephone service and costs; customer/telephone number; secretaries/receptionists names. (All record cards must be complete at all times.) Most suitable times for telephone bookings	Telephone techniques Listening technique	
	1.3 To write letters to book appointments	Letter construction Company procedures	Letter writing	
	1.4 To use diary to record appointments and work schedule	Diary record system		

Figure 3.6 Extract from job specification drawn up by the Chemical and Allied Products Industry Training Board

Functional analysis

Functional analysis has been defined by Lloyd and Cook (1993) as a 'technique for arranging a hierarchy of functions so that you can best describe an occupational area from its overall purpose down to the individual contributions needed for the fulfillment of that purpose'. This brings together all of the interactions that take place between work, workers and the organization. Therefore such an analysis involves input and commitment from staff at all levels to ensure that every job and each task within it are related to the ultimate purpose or function of the organization as a whole. It is another way of arriving at a job description.

This form of analysis is very much a 'top down' approach and should begin by establishing what the organization's function or key purpose is. For example, the key purpose of an electrical manufacturing company might be 'Supply a range of domestic electrical kitchen products to meet current and estimated future needs'. The next stage in the analysis would be to identify all of the different occupations within the organization. These could include sales, manufacturing, distribution, after-sales service, finance etc, all of which should be linked to the organization's key purpose by a key purpose of their own. For example, the key purpose of the distribution department might be: 'Coordinate and plan the dispatch of products to retail outlets to enable them to respond promptly to customer needs'. Further down the line, individuals will have a key purpose for each of their key roles and functions. For example, a packer in the distribution department could have a key purpose of 'Protect electrical goods with pre-formed polystyrene packaging to prevent damage in transit'. As each function or job is analyzed, its main components can be grouped together into Units which can be broken down further into Elements which relate very closely to actual work practices.

Having established the structure of the key roles, the analysis can be taken further to identify the scope of the tasks which is described in terms of Range Statements. These statements list the different conditions which might apply to the performance of a task. For example, the packer described earlier may have to use different types of protective material for a range of different items such as toasters, microwave ovens, washing machines etc. In order to ensure that the task is done properly a set of performance criteria are identified which list what is expected in the way of competent performance. Again, in the example of the packer, it would be expected that there would be reference to the appropriate pre-formed material being selected, where protective material is located in or around the equipment etc. The process of breaking down a key role or function into its component parts is likely to draw upon a number of analytical techniques. At the outset, brainstorming can be used to define key purposes. As the analysis becomes more detailed then some form of hierarchical task analysis or procedural analysis are likely to be of use. Both of these techniques are described in the following pages.

Hierarchical task analysis

Hierarchical task analysis is a technique developed by Annett and Duncan (1967) which has the advantage of being applicable to a wide range of jobs. It is a process by which tasks can be broken down into operations and sub- operations and presented in a format which resembles a family tree of all the duties, tasks and sub-tasks that make up a job or a main task within it (Figure 3.7)
It is not crucial to use the same terminology used in Figure 5.3; the important factor here is to understand the concept of breaking down tasks level by level so that the operations which make it up can be identified clearly. The example at Figure 3.7 illustrates the value and flexibility of using this technique. It is noticeable that all of the words used to describe the operations at each level of the hierarchy are 'behavioral'; that is, they describe what the operator actually does rather than give a general heading for the activity. The description 'Change engine oil' is of far more use than 'Engine oil'. While it is accepted that in this instance 'Engine oil' could give a clear idea of what is required, it is good practice always to use verbs so that there is no chance of confusion.

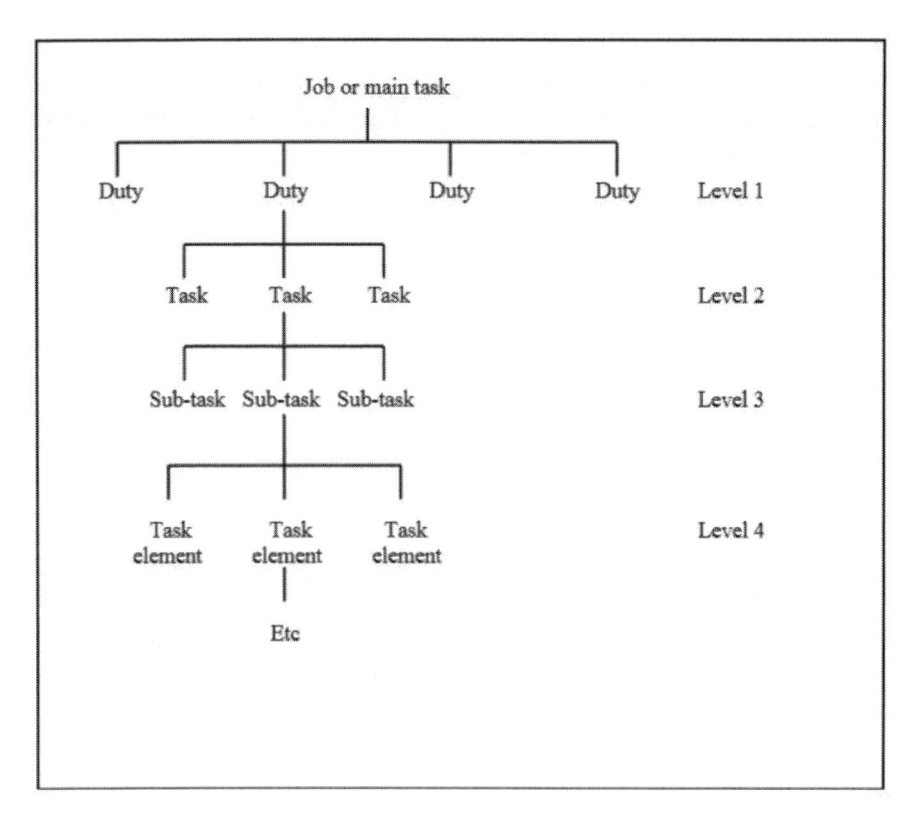

```
                        Job or main task
        ┌───────────┬───────┴───────┬───────────┐
       Duty        Duty            Duty        Duty         Level 1
                    │
              ┌─────┼─────┐
             Task  Task  Task                               Level 2
                    │
              ┌─────┼─────┐
          Sub-task Sub-task Sub-task                        Level 3
                    │
              ┌─────┼─────┐
             Task  Task  Task                               Level 4
           element element element
                    │
                   Etc
```

Figure 3.7 Family tree or hierarchy of tasks

Another feature of the hierarchy is that activities can be arranged sequentially when it is needed. The analysis of changing engine oil (Figure 3.8) provides a suggested sequence in which the tasks are carried out. Hierarchical task analysis is valuable for the trainer because it can present the job in its entirety, it can give a picture of the simplicity or complexity of the job, it helps to identify tasks and jobs which overlap (eg a number of tasks and more than one job may involve operating a photocopier) and because tasks can be presented sequentially it provides an aid to the learning process without reference to the principles of learning. A problem which trainers have encountered in using this technique is knowing when to stop analyzing. It has been envisaged that tasks could be analyzed down the levels ad infinitum. In many cases it becomes obvious when to stop and it is not unusual to see some tasks which do not have to be analyzed further than sub-task level while others need more in-depth treatment. It is useful in these instances to 'rule off' or to indicate in some other way that the analysis is complete. This overcomes the problem which might arise later of not knowing whether that part of the analysis has been finished.

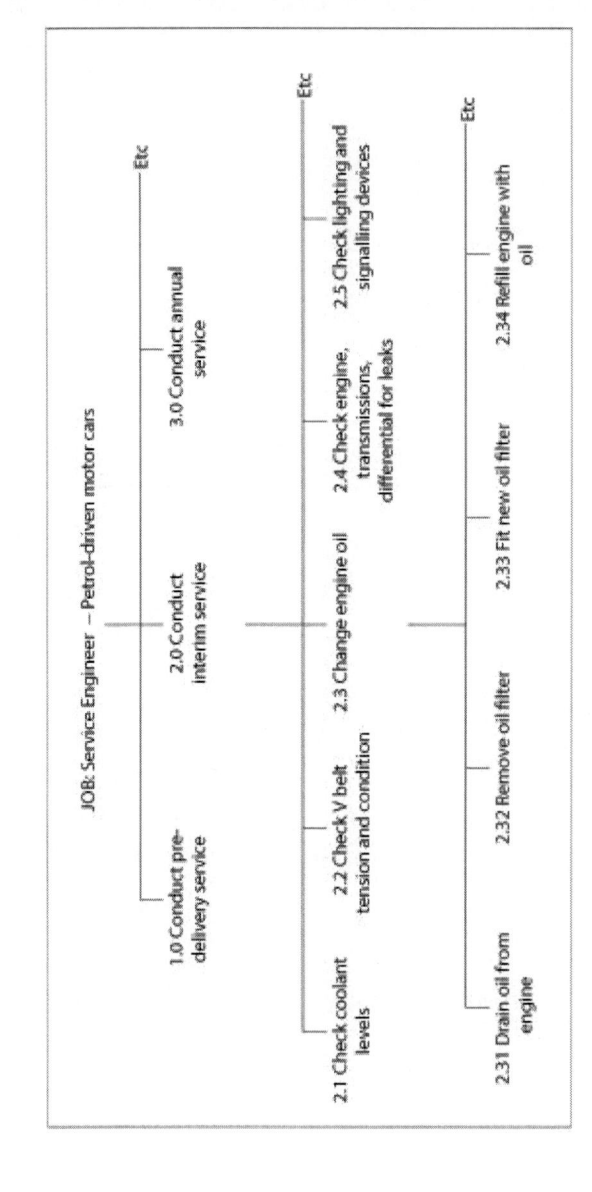

Figure 3.8 Example of hierarchical task analysis

Apart from the detail contained in the hierarchical diagram, it is quite likely that a number of supplementary notes and observations will be made. In order to avoid cluttering the diagram and causing confusion, notes can be kept as separate documents and numbers or some other form of coding can be used on the diagram as a reference. This information could include references to operating manuals, to legislation, to job aids, to other forms of analysis, etc. Annett and Duncan suggest two criteria to judge how far the analysis should go. Each operation should be looked at in terms of:

- What is the probability without training of inadequate performance?
- What would be the costs to the system of inadequate performance?

The probability of failure on each performance or operation is represented by P and the cost of inadequate performance is represented by C. The decision is made by examining the criteria in terms of P × C and when the outcome is considered to be unacceptable then the analysis should continue.

It has been shown how hierarchical task analysis can indicate the sequence of tasks and sub-tasks when those tasks are ordered serially. However, not all tasks follow a serial pattern and there are points within the hierarchy when the trainer may need to continue the analysis in a different format. This happens when there is no predetermined sequence and when the job holder is faced with circumstances which involve decision making which could result in any of a number of options being taken. The algorithm or decision tree has been found to be a useful way of recording this data. The example at Figure 3.9 illustrates this technique.

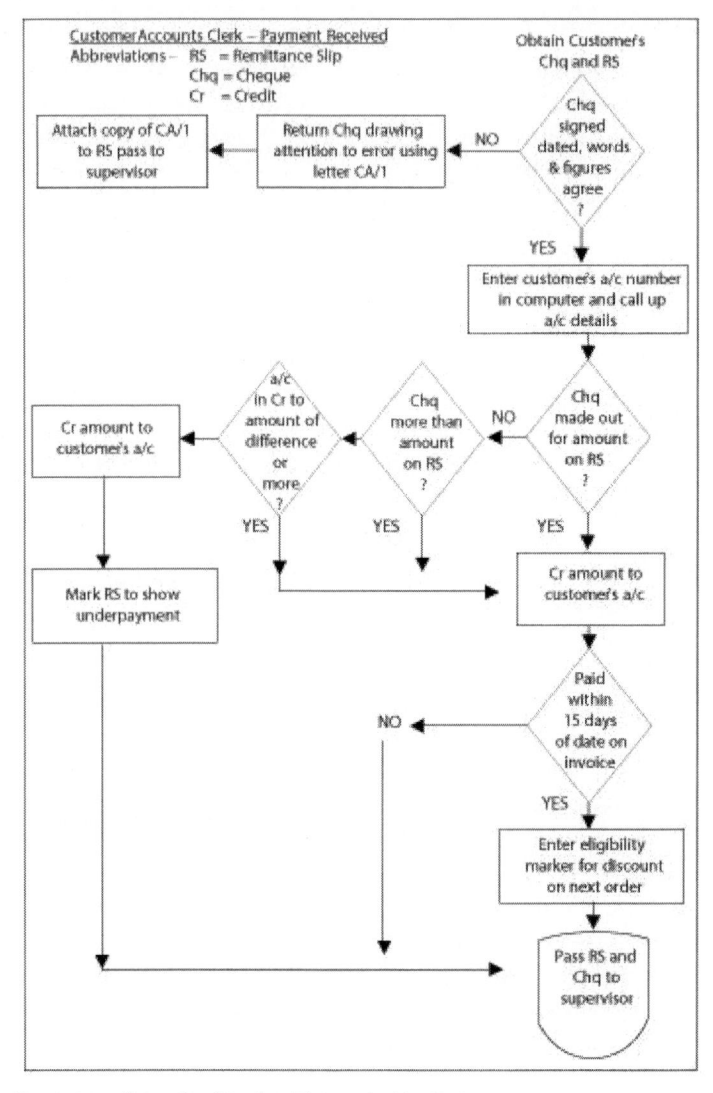

Figure 3.9 Example of an algorithm or decision tree

The technique can be extended to apply to procedures where there is more than one person involved in the operation. For example, in a production process an item may be passed through a number of operators before it is complete. This could involve finishers, checkers, etc. In the same way documents can be handled by a number of people before the procedure has been completed. Using the decision tree, links can be made between the work of different operators which might help to reveal problem areas in the procedure, eg too many links in the chain rather than performance problems on the part of the individual or individuals. An example of how jobs can be linked is shown in an extract from a decision tree in Figure 4.0

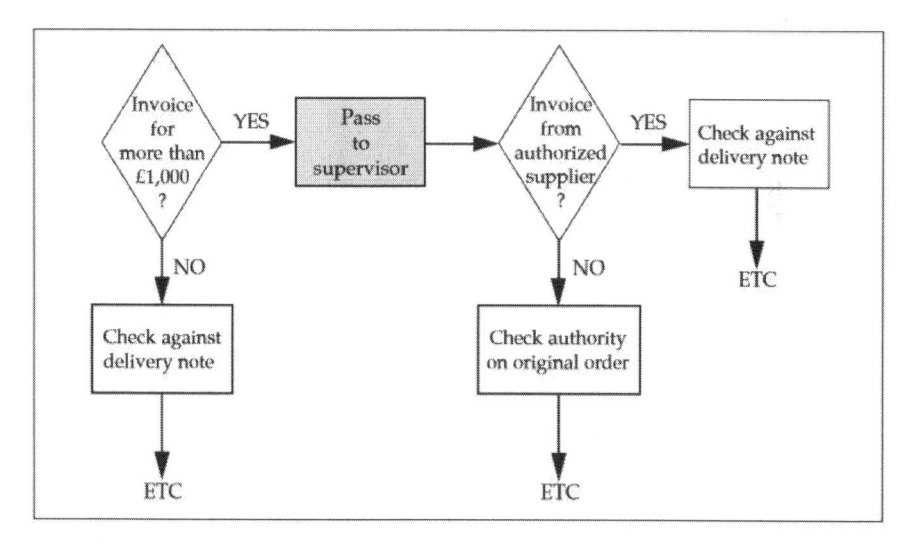

Figure 4.0 Example of algorithm/decision tree showing link between jobs

Key points analysis

This form of analysis is suitable for straightforward jobs and simple tasks for which no great amount of time needs to be spent on training. The outcome of such an analysis could be a simple job aid for the job holder or a guide for consumers similar to those issued with self-assembly products. The analysis focuses on three main aspects of a task – the sequence or stages in which it is performed, the instructions which describe how the task is done and the key points which have to be emphasized so that the operator does not make mistakes. All of this information can be presented in the form of a chart as shown in Figure 4.1

Task: How to wrap a parcel containing glassware		
Stage	Instructions	Key points
Pack glass item in protective cylinder	Place cylinder upright on a firm surface	Ensure cylinder is big enough to include sufficient polystyrene packing
	Seal top with card insert	
	Reverse cylinder	
	Put 5 cm layer of polystyrene chips in base	
	Insert glass item	
	Fill around and over glass item	Make sure adequate packing is placed around the item
	Seal with card insert	
Wrap in brown paper	Place sheet of paper on table	
etc		

Figure 4.1 Example of key points analysis

Faults analysis

Faults analysis could be used as part of a more detailed form of analysis or it could be used in its own right when the trainer is operating in a reactive mode in response to investigating performance problems as a result of feedback on quality control, customer complaints, etc. In the first of these two approaches the trainer is usually concerned with analyzing where problem areas are likely to occur, what the causes are likely to be, what might be the consequences of error and how the faults can be prevented. In this respect the trainer is being proactive, up to a point, and subsequently will be able to build into any job aids, training guides or lesson notes as indicators which will give advance warning to the trainees of possible problems, the symptoms of the problem and the appropriate action to take or what to do to prevent it from happening. This might be presented in the form of a faults specification as either a table or as a decision tree or algorithm. A number of motoring manuals contain a form of faults specification as a self-help guide to motorists (Figure 4.2)

Symptom	Cause	Remedy	Preventive measure
Brakes pull to one side	Soft tyre on one side	Check pressure and adjust	Check and adjust pressure weekly and before long journeys
	Worn or contaminated brake linings	Overhaul brakes	Ensure vehicle is serviced regularly

Figure 4.2 Example of faults specification

DIF (difficulty, importance, frequency) analysis

This form of analysis helps the trainer to decide between the 'need to know' and the 'nice to know' content of training. In its simple form (Figure 4.3) it could be used to help to decide how far one should continue with the hierarchical task analysis. It can be seen from the diagram that there are three criteria by which the decision to train is made – the level of difficulty of the task, the importance which is placed on it and the frequency with which it is performed. The diagram shows that when a task is difficult, important and performed frequently then training must be given. By contrast, when a task is not difficult, not important and performed infrequently then there is no need to train because it is quite likely that it can be learned while doing the job. One task which is worthy of note, is the task which is difficult, important but not performed frequently. The diagram indicates that in these circumstances the trainee should be over trained. This does not suggest an unnecessary amount of training which one might associate with overtraining. In this case it indicates that because the task is performed infrequently, the trainee must be trained to such a level in terms of skill or knowledge retention that there is little chance of under- performance when the event occurs. Emergency procedures would fall into this category.

Naturally, not every task needs to be measured against these criteria. In many cases the 'train' or 'no training' decision is clear. DIF analysis is a useful tool when the decisions are difficult to make and represents an approach for the trainer rather than a set of rules.

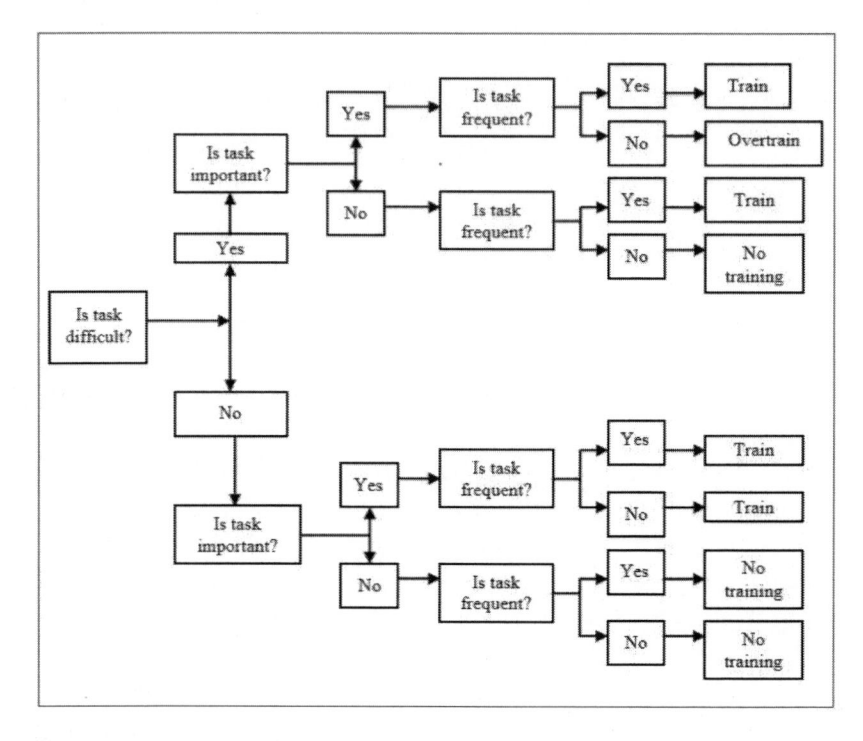

Figure 4.3 Example of DIF (difficulty, importance, frequency) analysis

The DIF analysis technique can be enhanced by building in different degrees of difficulty, importance and frequency and by introducing levels of training which give, for each task, an indication of the priority and the standard to be achieved. Figure 4.4 provides an example which has been developed from the basic model.

The levels of training shown in Figure 4.4 are shown on a scale of 1–5.

Level 1 indicates a very high priority for training to a standard which will ensure that a high level of skill and knowledge is retained without the job being done frequently. In effect this is 'overtraining'.

Level 2 sets a high priority for training to a standard of competence that will ensure that the task can be done without further training.

Level 3, being the midpoint of the scale, sets the priority level at average and to a standard which will ensure that the task is done efficiently. Further training or practice would be required to enhance performance.

Level 4 sets a low priority for training at a standard which provides no more than a basis for on-job training and practice.

Level 5 indicates that no formal training is required and that the task should be easy to learn whilst doing the job.

One of the problems which the trainer encounters in applying this form of DIF analysis is deciding how difficult tasks are and their relative levels of importance. Job holders and their supervisors often see the job from different perspectives and there is always the tendency for all job holders to enhance the importance of their jobs. The degree of importance which is attributed to any particular job or task needs to be measured against specific criteria; these might include danger to life, costs of failure to the organization, etc. Care has to be exercised in assessing level of difficulty because the skilled, long-serving operator could have forgotten how difficult the tasks were for him to learn. Similarly, some job holders may feel that it is a reflection on their performance if they admit that a task is difficult or that they do not do it. Sometimes the trainer will have to apply considerable skill in questioning to assess tasks at the correct level and continually focus on 'what do you think a newcomer to the job would find difficult?' The degrees of difficulty, importance and frequency also need to be decided carefully by the trainer. There is no set scale which can be applied to all situations.

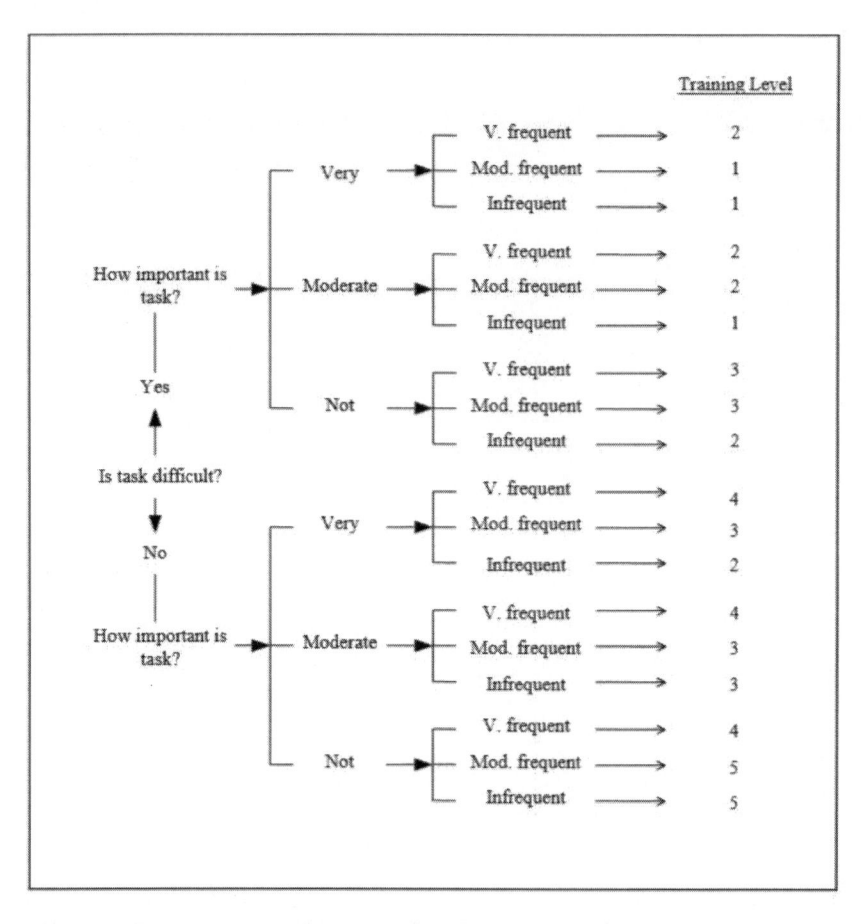

Figure 5.10 Example of DIF analysis and levels of training

The data needed to complete a DIF analysis can be obtained from job holders, recent trainees and supervisors using interviews and questionnaires. Some of the information may have been obtained at an earlier stage in the investigation. The outcome is that the trainer is in a better position to make decisions on the content and design of training, the allocation of resources to priorities and the standards which must be set as a target for training.

Critical incident technique

This form of analysis or technique for gathering information can be used within the process of most of the forms of analysis that have been described so far. It is a procedure developed by Flanagan (1954) for collecting information about incidents which have proved to be critical to the effective performance of a job; that is, incidents that have contributed directly to success or failure. It has been a useful tool when conducting a DIF (difficulty, importance, frequency) analysis and when there is a need to separate a large number of activities which are all seen by the job holder as having a high level of importance. It is particularly valuable when constraints on training time force the trainer to concentrate on the vital or critical aspects of job performance. Similarly, it is of value when studying tasks that are not performed frequently, such as emergency procedures, or which cannot be observed directly because of physical constraints or lack of access to the job environment, such as working in a confined space. Information can best be collected by individual and group interviews. A pre- formatted response sheet might also be used but this could prove difficult if the trainer does not have sufficient knowledge of the job. Using a tape recorder during interview sessions ensures that the flow of description is not inhibited by the trainer trying to make copious notes. Those participating should be asked to describe incidents which have resulted in success or failure in achieving job objectives, to place these incidents into a context and to relate precisely what they did to bring about the successful or unsuccessful outcome. For example, the failure to ask probing questions at a critical point in a disciplinary interview could lead to problems with industrial relations.

Similarly, failure to check a replacement part number for a piece of sensitive equipment could lead to costly damage. On the more positive side, being alert to the need to ask probing questions and to check part numbers could be seen as critical for a successful outcome. It follows that there is likely to be a natural reluctance on the part of individuals to 'confess' to the remainder of the group, or in private, that they have made bad mistakes. Therefore, confidentiality must be guaranteed for all participants. Once the information has been gathered it can be categorized as appropriate to the needs of the study and checklists can be produced for further investigation. However, the categorization of all data based on anecdotal experience is liable to be subjective to a greater or lesser degree and it is important that trainers are in agreement over their approach, especially as they will need to record and categorize a large number of incidents in order to gain a clear picture of the job that they are analyzing.

Repertory grid technique

This form of analysis or technique is similar to the critical incident technique in that it examines and compares good with poor performance. The repertory grid technique can be used in a number of ways. These include:

- identifying training needs;
- evaluating the success of training courses;
- exploring management's opinion of the training function;
- examining the marketing of training products and services.

The technique is based on a system which examines what have been called personal constructs or ways in which we view the world. The repertory grid is a method in which these constructs can be drawn out. As with the critical incident technique, the interview is the tool by which the trainer obtains the information to build up the grid. However, the interview is much more highly structured and interviewers need to be well-trained in order to avoid the bias that could be placed unwittingly on the responses given by the interviewees. This technique is particularly useful in probing the areas of interpersonal skills and, unlike some other techniques; a considerable amount of information can be gathered from a small number of people. Interviewees are asked to think carefully of aspects of job performance which are referred to as elements. Basically the elements chosen should depend on the purpose of the study or project being undertaken. However, beyond this general criterion, there are several guidelines for selecting specific elements:

- Use objects, people, events or activities and make them as discrete as possible.
- Do not mix classes of elements; objects, people, events or activities should not be muddled up.

- Do not have an element as a part or sub-set of another element, eg tea as one element and darjeeling tea as another element.
- Avoid elements that are evaluative or might be construed in an evaluative way, eg involvement, controlling, etc.
- Do not use abstract nouns, eg 'the perfect boss'.

The elements for a training manager could be the trainers or instructors for whom he or she is responsible. In order to examine the nature of good and poor performance as an instructor or tutor, the following procedure should be followed with the tutors:

- Write the name of each instructor or tutor on a card and arrange the cards into two piles. One pile should contain the names of those who are good at their job and the other pile should consist of those who are not as good or poor at their job.
- Two names are selected from the 'good' pile and one name from the 'poor/ bad' pile so that comparisons can be made between them. First, those who have been described as good are compared for similarities and then they are compared with the less able performer for differences.
- Having noted the differences the next stage is what is called laddering. This involves picking out specific behaviors which are important to the job in the eyes of the interviewee and probing each one for detailed information. This will identify the key behaviors which contribute to good performance. This stage is vital if we are to avoid vague statements which cannot be used for any practical purpose.

Knowledge and topic analysis

In its simplest form, knowledge analysis involves supplying greater detail about the knowledge items in the job specification. This additional information may need to be presented in the form of notes, diagrams, maps, photographs, samples, procedural sequences, etc.

A more complex form of knowledge analysis is that of topic analysis which, in addition to factual information, covers comprehension and intellectual skill. A variant of topic analysis has been described by Davies (1971). In this analysis, a topic is first broken down into its smallest constituent parts or elements and these are then set out in a hierarchical form. It is important to limit the topic and to try to ensure that it is as self-contained as possible.

Davies refers to the elements making up a topic as 'rules'. A rule is basically 'a statement of generality, a definition, a factor, an item of information'. He suggests that to identify the rules, which form the building blocks of a topic, the analyst should ask the following questions:

- What does the analyst expect the trainee to do to demonstrate that he has learned the topic?
- What questions does the analyst expect the trainee to answer?
- What tasks, procedures and techniques does the analyst expect the trainee to perform, and to what standard of performance?
- What discriminations does the analyst expect and in what terms does he or she expect these discriminations to be made?
- What total changes in behavior are expected and how will they be observed and measured?

In addition, Davies emphasizes the importance of ensuring that the rules are carefully written and sequenced and that they:
- comprise only a single factor or idea;
- are composed at the same level of generality as preceding rules;
- take the form of simple, core sentences;
- avoid negative forms, qualifications and conjunctions;
- contain only one active verb;
- are critical and essential to performing the task

Every effort should be made to ensure that the rules follow a logical and natural sequence, each rule leading on to the next in an easily understandable way. Davies points out that the traditional 'laws' of sequence should be borne in mind when arranging the order which the rules should take, ie:

- Proceed from known to unknown.
- Proceed from the simple to the complex.
- Proceed from the concrete to the abstract.
- Proceed from observation to reasoning.
- Proceed from a whole view to a more detailed view to a whole view.

Cognitive analysis

Cognitive task analysis (CTA) is a relatively new development which goes beyond traditional forms of analyses, ie knowledge, skills and attitudes. As Salas and Cannon-Bowers (2001) point out, CTA '. . . refers to a set of procedures for understanding the mental processing and mental requirements for job performance' and that training needs analysis should not only identify the necessary knowledge and specific skills required to perform tasks effectively but in addition, should identify '. . . the cues and cognitions that enable trainees to know when to apply those skills.'

CTA is conducted by asking subject matter experts and novice workers to describe what they are doing and why. In other words, get them to think aloud while they are performing a task. It focuses on how experts differ from novices in the manner in which they make critical decisions in natural settings. In this way mind maps, algorithms and decision trees can be drawn up and used as job or training aids to help trainees until such time as they can perform the tasks automatically or instinctively. Goldstein and Ford (2002) point out, in summarizing the research on expert-novice differences, experts can see the 'wood for the trees', and for them the pieces making up a task are more structured and integrated. In addition, referring to a study by Gitomer (1988), they highlight that experts '. . . use mental models that were much more consistent with the true functional properties of the trouble shooting task.'

Developing training program that take account of the mental processes, models and strategies employed by experts should help trainees to accelerate their learning and ensure that the training is carried out more efficiently in terms of time and resources. A study undertaken on weapons engineers in the Royal Netherlands Navy by Schaafstal, Schraagen and van Berlo (2000), which resulted in a new method of training being introduced, supports this conclusion. They compared traditional and new training courses on trouble shooting for novice naval technicians. To begin with the researchers considered the differences in trouble shooting between experts and novices. Using a form of CTA they discovered that the experienced technicians approached matters in a more systematic way, mentally represented the systems they were examining more authentically and at several levels of abstraction, and employed more efficient strategies than their less experienced colleagues. In contrast the novices suffered from information overload and a lack of understanding of the functions and systems involved, and had not developed adequate strategies to undertake the troubleshooting procedures effectively. The design of the new training course was based on the observations made on expert technicians and on expert-novice differences highlighted above. The results obtained through the new course compared with the traditional course were unambiguous. On the new course trainee technicians solved twice as many malfunctions, over a shorter period, as those trained on the old program. Furthermore, the new training course was completed in less time than the traditional one.

Manual skills analysis

This form of analysis is used to examine those tasks which involve a high degree of manual dexterity and perception. It has a wide range of application and could be used to analyze the skills used, for example, by a lathe operator, a word-processor operator or someone working in the crafts such as weaving, pottery, etc. In these skills the analyst would observe and record the movements of the hands, the fingers, the eyes and other senses. Examples of the use of the senses in the practice of skills include taste for wine connoisseurs, hearing for musicians, touch for pastry cooks to gauge the consistency of dough, etc. The concept of dexterity can be extended to include the use of the feet. The operator of a crawler crane is likely, in some of the maneuvers he has to perform, to use hands and feet to drive and to operate the gib, vision to gauge the position of the gib and attachments such as buckets or hooks, the vision to look out for signals from those guiding operations, hearing to listen for the note of the engine, etc.

All of these movements and sensory functions can be recorded in a tabular format, the layout of which will depend on the skills which have to be analyzed. The analysis of a carpenter's skill shown at Figure 4.5 is presented purely as an illustration of how the technique can be used and is not taken from any training document.

Task: Cut timber to size					
Task element	Left hand	Right hand	Vision	Other senses	Comments
Select piece of timber	Reach to pile of prepared timber, grasp with 1, 2, 3, 4 and T and place on top of bench		Confirm timber not damaged or warped	Touch – either hand to confirm timber is smooth	Unaccepted timber placed on reject pile
Measure and mark timber	Grasp measure 1, 2, 3, 4 on top T underneath and place on timber	Grasp pencil 1, 2 and T and mark timber at appropriate length	Check measure placed at end of timber, identify specified distance on measure. Confirm pencil mark on correct position		
Place saw in position to cut timber etc	Palm on flat surface of timber	Grasp saw 2, 3, 4 and T around hand grip. 1 along side of handgrip pointing forward. Place saw on pencil mark	Confirm saw in correct position		

Note: T = thumb; 1, 2, 3, 4 = fingers

Figure 5.4 Example of manual skills analysis

Social skills analysis

In examining interpersonal or social skills it may be necessary to undertake some form of behavior analysis. This involves classifying ongoing social interactions into discrete oral and non-verbal units or elements. The purpose of this type of analysis is to identify those behaviors that constitute effective and ineffective performance in particular social situations. Rackham and Morgan (1977) describe a methodology for arriving at such critical behaviors.

The application of their methodology begins by developing a behavior analysis system which is appropriate to the social situation that is being examined.

it should be noted that the non-verbal categories are not included in Rackham and Morgan's list. There then need to be developed the criteria or measures that could be used to pinpoint individuals in that social situation whose performances are regarded either as effective or ineffective. It is then possible to identify and to observe particular individuals who are seen as high and low performers when measured against the criteria. The behavior analysis schema can be used either to record or to describe the frequency of incidence of the different behaviors. From this the critical behavioral dimensions, that help to distinguish high and low performers, can be identified. For example, Rackham and Carlisle (1978) identify the behaviors that characterize skilled negotiators as being: behavior labeling, testing understanding, summarizing, seeking information, feelings commentary, etc. By contrast the less skilled or average negotiator tends to use: irritators, counter proposals, defend/attack spirals. The one-to-one or group situations in which the above type of analysis might be applicable include: interviewing – selection, discipline, appraisal, counsel- ling; coaching and training (including telephone sales); group problem-solving; team negotiation; chairing meetings.

Evaluating criteria

Besides being concerned with the standards set on the criteria, the trainer must ensure also that the criteria are adequate in a number of specific ways. They must be relevant, free from contamination, not deficient in any respect and they must be reliable. These requirements have been discussed by Goldstein (1986) and are described briefly below:

Criterion relevance is the degree to which the criteria employed to assess the effectiveness of training during and after the event clearly relate, directly or indirectly, to the relevant knowledge, skills and attitudes, task/task elements and pertinent organizational outcomes, identified through earlier analysis, ie job analysis, topic and skills analysis, etc. Figure 4.6 illustrates these relation- ships.

During and on the completion of training

Acquisition or achievement of knowledge, skills, attitudes and other outcomes, eg outputs

After training

Performance of task/task elements

Specific results, organizational goals etc

Application of training criteria

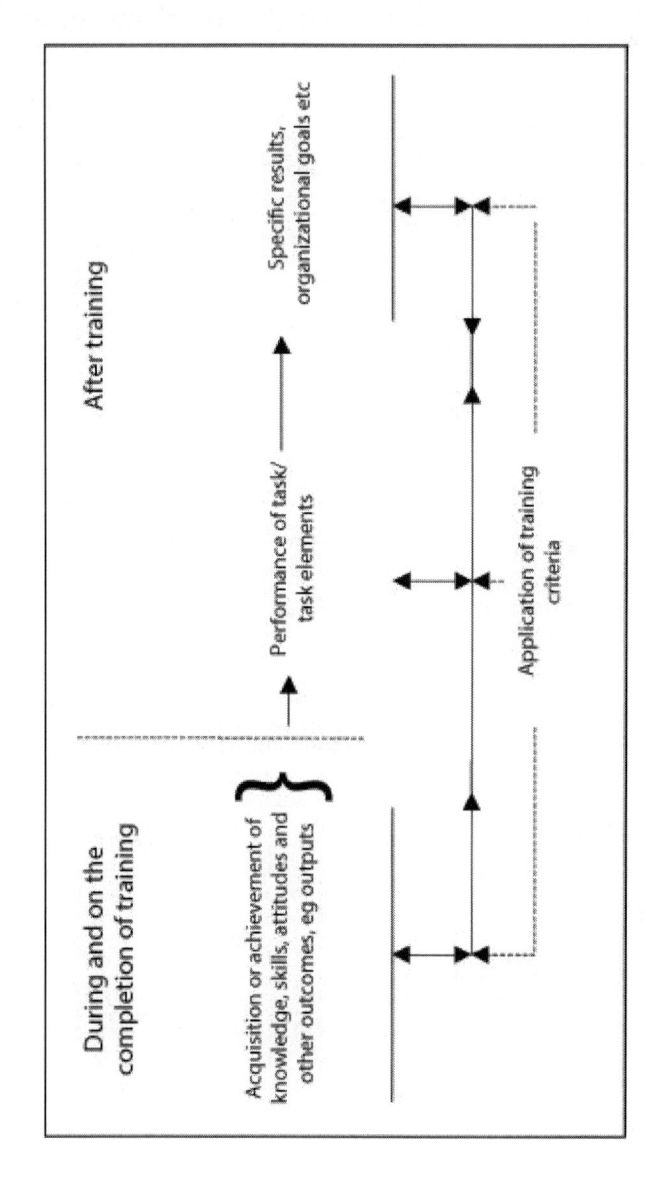

Figure 4.6 Relationships between factors affecting criteria relevance

Thus, for example, the knowledge, skill, attitude and output criteria selected or developed for application during and on completion of training are only pertinent to the extent that they reflect the equivalent components on the tasks that need the training treatment. Failure to meet the above conditions of fidelity leads to either criterion deficiency or criterion contamination. Criterion deficiency is concerned with the extent to which the actual criteria employed at various points 'fall short' of the potentially relevant criteria identified in the training needs assessment. Such a situation may occur for two possible reasons. The training need covered on the training program, expressed in terms of either knowledge, skill or attitude, is not included in the on-training or on-job criterion construct, or the training need is not included in the training program at all. Criterion contamination occurs when extraneous elements or influences are present in the criterion which result in the measure not representing faithfully the factor identified in the training needs analysis. For instance, if a trainee's supervisor knows how well he or she has performed on the training course this may bias, favorably or unfavorably, the supervisor's assessment of the trainee's subsequent on-job performance. A fundamental requirement of any criterion is reliability. Given the same instrument or means of assessment, criterion reliability refers to either how consistent the measure on the criterion is over time, or to the degree of agreement between two or more ostensibly similar methods of assessing the initial position or change on the criterion. For example, in the latter case, poor agreement between two raters making independent judgments of a trainee's performance in a particular skill would indicate low reliability. Low criterion reliability would cast doubt not only on the means of assessment employed but also on the supposed effects of different forms of training treatment or non- treatment.

Chapter 10: Delivering Training

Having designed the training it is important to deliver it effectively. If you are regularly delivering training, you will be aware of many of the points that make for effective delivery; however, if you are new to training you should prepare very carefully. No trainer or line manager should attempt to run a formal training session without being trained themselves. Most companies run train-the-trainer program for their internal trainers, or there are external providers your style of delivery will very much depend on the type of event you are planning. As a trainer you will be performing a number of roles: direct training, one-to-one coaching, facilitating and/or presenting at a conference.

We will look at delivering a training program. If the program has been carefully designed, your life as a trainer will be much easier. You should be supported with all the material necessary to run the event. There are a number of key stages within the delivery process.

If you are an experienced trainer or have conducted training sessions before, you may skip this chapter.

Before the event

Ensure that all participant material is completed and ready for use. Your trainer's guide should be complete with your guidance notes computer-generated presentations, videos and other supporting material.

Take time to run through the content. Some trainers like to make additional notes to support their presentation. Always make sure that these are written large enough to be read at a distance. Start each key area with a new page, or a new card, and always number the pages. Sometimes, if people are delivering a formal presentation, they will use postcards with key points written on them. Again either join them together with a tag or number the cards. Prepare a box containing all the support material that you may need. Sample contents could be:

- pads, pens, tent cards/name badges for the learners;

- spare flipchart paper: if you are using a hotel check what they are supplying;
- marker pens, Blu-Tack®, masking tape;
- A4 paper for individual and group activities;
- stapler and staples, paperclips, Post-it® notes, scissors, glue, rubber, ruler, pencils, pencil sharpener;
- other items specific to group activities, eg rewards, prizes for games; some corporate events include larger gifts for team games;
- promotional material, such as pens, hats, T-shirts, polo shirts and other branded goods, which are sometimes requested at team events; these need to be ordered in good time with sizes checked and agreed prior to the event.

Ensure that the venue has been booked and that a letter with the details of the timetable, start and finish times, refreshment breaks, any special dietary needs and the equipment requirements is sent either to the external venue or to an internal facilities manager.

If you or the learners need overnight accommodation ensure it is booked and confirmation is received. Take time to run through the program and have prepared any additional notes or comments to support your delivery.

Ensure that you and your learners have a letter with full details of the day's timetable, the venue, maps and directions, any special clothing required (eg if there are leisure activities ensure that people know so that they can bring the correct clothing). Also people should be told if dress is to be casual during the day, or semi-formal in the evening.

Prior to the event you should also decide what you are going to wear so that if anything needs cleaning, or you want to buy something new, everything is organized in plenty of time. Trainers often move from hotel to hotel, in and out of cars, airplanes, so investing in easy-care, coordinated outfits makes life much easier. Equally you often need clothes that are defined as 'smart casual'. As a trainer you are often very active, so wear things that look smart and professional but are also comfortable. Some trainers also take a spare shirt/blouse to change into during the day, usually the same color. Alternatively, they travel in very casual clothes and change once they have set up the room, so they feel fresh at the start of the event.

Always allow plenty of time to travel to the event and have a back-up route planned. Consider staying at the venue the night before if there is a chance that you may not arrive in time, or you will have to get up so early to reach it that you will be tired during the day.

The night before the event work through the program session by session. You will often find that fresh points occur to you. Make additional notes in your trainer's guide if you feel they are important. Resist massive re-scripting at this stage.

Finally, relax, do something that you enjoy and go to bed at a reason- able time, having set up an early morning call or alarm and booked a taxi if required, or checked the car for petrol, etc.

On the morning of the event

Arrive with time to set up the room. Normally, the room will already be arranged in the formation you requested, but often some of the finer details may not have been understood. Sometimes the instruction has not been given to the relevant people and there is a degree of furniture moving to be undertaken. Always elicit support if it is available.

Ensure that all the equipment works. Be particularly sure to check computer and projector are working, check the light conditions and if it will affect the projector or not.

Lay out the material for learners, including the learner guide, pads, pens, tent cards and/or name badges. Make it look welcoming and inviting.

It is often easier to prepare your first few flipcharts beforehand. Include an initial message, such as 'Welcome to... [insert title of your program]'. Write your name on the corner of the page, or on a tent card at the front of the room, or put on a name badge.

Check on the arrangements for the coffee/tea on arrival and that water/fruit juices/squash are on the learners' tables. Where possible arrange for all-day refreshments. This means that you can take shorter but more frequent breaks without having to wait for the arrival of refreshments. Giving learners regular breaks often helps with the learning process.

The delivery

When you are ready and it is the correct starting time, encourage the learners into the room and welcome them to the event. Always try to start promptly or if you know some learners are delayed, tell the rest of the group and arrange a new start time. It is often better to start and allow latecomers to join the group than keep people hanging around. Ensure you spend time with those who arrive late helping them to catch up with the key information they have missed.

Sometimes you may have a senior person to open the event. Ideally, ask them to do their input first so that you can then run the rest of the program without interruption. Hopefully they will be motivational and helpful in setting the tone for the day.

At the beginning of your input you need to introduce yourself, list the procedures to be followed in the event of an emergency and give other domestic details like the location of washroom facilities.

Follow this by encouraging people to write their names on tent cards. Do not assume that if they are from one organization they automatically know each other. Even if they do know each other it is quite in order to say, 'It would help me if you could all briefly introduce yourselves and say a little about your experience.' Normally this can be structured by asking for the following:

- o name;
- o job title;
- o years of experience; and
- o any previous training attended.

It is important to try to learn the learners' names. If you have a problem remembering names try to find a way of overcoming this. The following points may help:

- As the learners introduce themselves jot down brief details about them in the same formation as the seating. This can also help later in the day when you are dividing them into syndicate groups and you want each group to contain a range of expertise.
- Some people reinforce their recollection of people's names by repeating the names several times in the initial conversation, eg thanking them by name for their contribution.
- Talking to people on a one-to-one basis during the breaks helps to add other pieces of information to their name.
- One well-known ice-breaker is to ask people to give the usual information and then to tell the group something unusual about them-selves that no one else knows, eg, 'My name is George and I breed green canaries.' It's a test of everyone's memory to repeat this later and to identify what the group can remember about these initial introductions.

Your style

However well the program has been designed it is the trainer(s) who bring it to life. As we discussed earlier, your role is critical to the success of the event.

You should encourage interaction, manage questions and help everyone to contribute and feel part of the event. While debate is an important part of the learning, you also have to oversee it to ensure that one or two learners do not control all of the discussion, leaving the rest of the group as observers.

The experienced trainer develops the ability to answer the questions, widen the debate to include others as appropriate and then to move on. If your program has been carefully timetabled, you will lose valuable time if you do not control the event, and then you lose respect from your group. Always acknowledge a good question and try to respond positively, even if it is a sensitive area. If you do not know the answer, or the questioner appears to want to monopolize the session, suggest that you discuss it with them later on a one-to-one basis.

Sometimes you may have to handle conflict, or facilitate the group to handle difficult situations. Always be sensitive. Recognize individual learning styles and the differing needs and experience of individuals.

During the event you should be ultra-observant, ensuring that the group stays with you and recognizing when someone is struggling or feeling uncomfortable. Take time during the breaks to get to know the person, and try to encourage them to articulate their concerns so that you can help them to overcome the issue, either during the program or after the event, perhaps through coaching. It is not appropriate to discuss potentially sensitive areas in front of an individual's peers, and you need to respect their need for privacy.

As a trainer you are in powerful position. <u>Never abuse it</u>. Instead, use your skill to work with all the members of the group while recognizing the different individual starting points. The more relaxed you are, the better you will be able to work with the group. If you are co-tutoring you must establish a way of working that lets you both use your individual strengths to facilitate the progress of the event.

The pace of the day should be carefully controlled to allow for maximum participation from the learners. It is important not to have too much input from the trainer at any one time; instead structure these slots throughout the day. Carefully watch your group for signs of boredom, discomfort or loss of involvement.

You also need to manage your own energy levels, as running training events can be exhausting. Eat and drink sensibly during the day to ensure a balanced sugar level. Sometimes trainers find themselves running out of energy or getting 'hyper' because they have eaten the wrong food or drunk too much coffee during the day. Five light snacks may be best for you, using fruit where possible. This is also important for learners. Try to avoid the provision of heavy lunches and encourage them to get some fresh air, which will help them to maintain concentration. (This does not mean a visit to the nearest coffee shop!)

If you have time, also take a break outside; it will help to clear your head from the morning's events. Use the time to review the progress of the group, either by yourself or with your co-tutor. Keep checking the temperature in the room during the day. Sometimes there is a build-up of heat as the day progresses, which results in the learners feeling lethargic.

Ending the event

Whether it has been a one-day program or a longer event, the key outcome should be that the learners are able to go back and do. If the objectives have been achieved, then the learners should be setting action plans ready to review them with their line managers.

Every training event should have a significant impact on the individual and the business. You want learners to leave feeling positive and motivated and not just on adrenalin 'high'.

Most trainers also finish with some opportunity for the learners to comment on their own personal learning experiences during the event.

Always thank the learners for their attendance, and ensure that you did meet the objectives and their needs. Highlight any follow-up training that has been organized, and offer a contact number for any individual follow-up needs.

After the learners have left, gather together all the materials and put them into the right order ready for filing or to be used again at another event. Check the syndicate rooms for any resources left behind. If you are writing a post-course report, remember to save any relevant flipcharts or other materials.

Organizing venues

Like speakers, organizing venues takes time and patience to get right, and often forms part of the trainer's role. If you have administrative back up, it is something that can be learnt once you have established the guide- lines. You need very clear criteria to help you identify your ideal venue.

First, identify what you require in terms of the venue, which will vary depending on your event. If it is an in-company program, you may have to use in-company facilities; however, increasingly organizations are prepared to use off-site facilities if they feel it is important to create different environments for the learning.

Main room

- Is it large enough, and well ventilated with natural light?
- Is the seating comfortable, with a facility for the learners to write on?
- Are there syndicate rooms nearby?
- Are there toilets nearby?
- Is there a business center, or somewhere where you can photocopy?
- Are there any likely planned disturbances, eg refurbishment, decorating or rebuilding?
- Are other large events being organized at the same time at the venue? (Sometimes small events can be overwhelmed by other, large conferences.)

Refreshments

- How are the refreshments organized? Will coffee/tea be available in the room? Can they be available all day if required?
- Is there a separate facility for a buffet lunch? Can you have part of the dining room kept separate for your group? This is particularly important for a residential event, where people prefer to eat together away from other guests. Some venues have private dining room facilities.

- What additional refreshments are available: mineral water, squash, mints, biscuits, cakes, fruit, etc? How are these items costed? What's included in the rate, what is additional? It is very important to establish the real costs when comparing one venue with another. Benchmark a variety of venues.

Handling learners' resistance or reluctance

Despite your best preparation and working in your most facilitative style, you may find yourself in a situation when you have to handle learner resistance. There may be a number of reasons for this:

- lack of notice about a training event or resentment at being 'sent';
- nervousness on learners' part about attending;
- not wanting to be 'shown up' in front of peers;
- personal reasons unrelated to the event;
- personal chemistry issues between learners, or between learners and the trainer;
- issues with the organization or the management.

Any of the above can create tensions within the learning environment/ training room. This may manifest itself in many ways, sometimes by a learner not getting involved in the course, or by a learner arriving late, wanting to leave early, or creating verbal challenges. A learner may show a lack of interest or possibly challenge the trainer, demonstrating 'When you cannot reach me, you cannot teach me.'

The event itself, including the trainer, can be questioned through comments such as, 'You don't understand our situation', 'Your examples wouldn't work in our set-up' or, 'This has been tried before and the management didn't follow it through.' The flow of a training session can be disrupted when learners want to vent their own issues.

The suggested strategies for coping with these situations are split over four areas.

1. before the training event:

Part of the pre-event planning should involve identification of any potential organizational issues. Talk to learners' managers, ensuring that the managers and the learners are clear about the importance of the course and that learners are being prepared appropriately. Discuss any potential issues with the managers, particularly if there are personal or organizational circumstances that may influence your event.

2. At the start of the event, in the training room

Establishing some ground rules at the start of the event can help in terms of mutual respect and support. Demonstrating that you understand organizational issues, being flexible and adaptable in the way that the course is structured, allowing regular breaks and organizing access to all-day refreshments will all help to create an environment that is conducive to learning and supportive to the learners. Simple strategies such as asking the learners what they hope to gain from the event should identify areas of common ground. This works best as an interactive session, writing up their suggestions on a flipchart and being very honest about what will be covered and what needs to be addressed outside of the event or potentially on a one-to one basis. Remember that this does imply a commitment to try to meet their needs. It is easy to fall into the trap of identifying their needs only to ignore their input and to carry on and deliver the content that you had in mind with no further reference to their ideas.

3. during the training event

Once the event has started, the intuitive trainer will be working to develop positive relationships with the group, recognizing when the group needs a break and all the issues about attention span. Hopefully in the design and planning of the event there will be variety in pace and content, but don't be afraid to change the plan if the learners are not responding positively. If you are co-tutoring, recognize the support that the other trainer can offer; by mixing and matching styles and approaches, the learners' interest can be maintained.

Once you understand the cause of resistance, you can plan to handle it. All trainers need to be aware of their own natural fears, including 'Am I good enough?', 'Have I the authority I need?' and 'They don't like me.' It is key not to take situations personally and to consider the reasons behind challenging situations. Experience helps with these situations, but first courses can be daunting – an excellent reason to run pilots and to build in feedback sessions within the event and, if possible, co-train with an experienced facilitator. Remember your sources of confidence, keep eye contact with your learners, move closer to them and discuss their issues. All our coping strategies rely on our ability to keep our cool and our ability to choose the appropriate response to the situation. Fear can result in our making the wrong choice.

If there is a general feeling of discontent or restlessness, be prepared to take time out to identify the cause. You may need to refer back to the objective and main agenda of the event including the learners' expressed needs and, adult to adult, seek to identify the reasons for lack of concentration and establish a joint commitment to work together to overcome any issues.

4. following the event

it is really important that you care- fully review all training events; as well as the formal evaluations, you should undertake your personal review or review the event with your co- trainer. You should always be running a 'sense check' during any event, recognizing the signals and trying to be in tune with the needs of the learners. Regularly discuss progress with the program sponsors and be open to any feedback that they have received. Equally, even with careful preparation and with all possible care on your part, there may be events that are less successful than others. The important factor is to learn from the experience, seek to identify areas for improvement, and work to make sure that at the next event the lessons learnt can be applied in the new context.

Lack of learners

Sometimes, for a variety of last-minute reasons, the numbers that turn up are severely reduced. One or two fewer people, or equally one or two more than are expected, should present no problem. However, a dramatic drop in numbers may mean that the program is no longer viable in terms of interaction or sharing of best practice. On these occasions you have to make a series of judgments:

- If the program is part of an internal roll-out program, are there others nearby who could be released to attend? Always clear this with their line managers.
- Has everyone arrived, are any just late?
- When is a group too small? It is possible to run an event with small numbers, but it is likely to be less effective, because people have less opportunity to share other people's experiences. Success also depends on your experience, as a more experienced trainer can turn a small group into a coaching session.

As a trainer you always have to be prepared for the unexpected, although most events happen without any problems. Preparation and identifying venues that are able to respond to your needs are the keys. It is essential to keep a balanced and professional approach, but if you do experience difficulties, ask to see the duty manager, who often will be able to solve them for you.

Chapter 11: Instructional Systems Design

So you done everything we talked about in the previous chapters, now we come to the most common thing that unfortunately many trainers out there have no knowledge about ISD or Instructional System Design.

ISD is the practice of creating "instructional experiences which make the acquisition of knowledge and skill more efficient, effective, and appealing. The process consists broadly of determining the current state and needs of the learner, defining the end goal of instruction, and creating some "intervention" to assist in the transition. Ideally the process is informed by pedagogically (process of teaching) and andragogically (adult learning) tested theories of learning and may take place in student-only, teacher-led or community-based settings. The outcome of this instruction may be directly observable and scientifically measured or completely hidden and assumed. There are many instructional design models but many are based on the ADDIE model with the five phases: analysis, design, development, implementation, and evaluation (Figure 4.7)

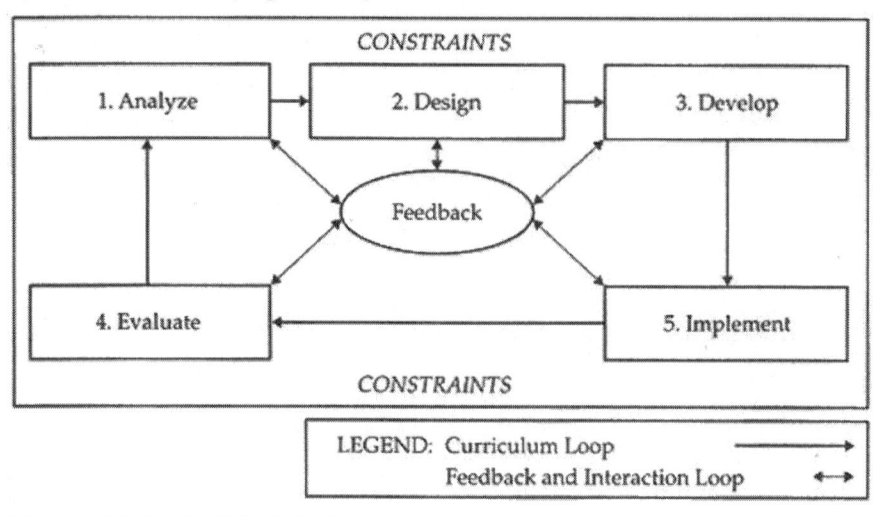

Figure 4.7 Basic ISD Model

Since its inception in the early 1960s, ISD has undergone very little change. ISD was designed to provide a template for the development of instruction by the U.S. military, where it remains the foundation for courseware. Recent discussions with educational researchers and users underscore the fact that the basic ISD model and its underlying systems approach are relevant and sound. ISD is used extensively in U.S. government agencies to develop courseware, especially for highly critical training. It is employed by utilities, process plants, and human health systems. Although the models employed by these users are highly elaborated, most training programs can use the basic model to provide an architectural blueprint or guide, ensuring that essential components have been addressed. Intrinsic to the ISD system is the ability to create an audit trail to evaluate and modify a program. ISD has been adapted for the development of multimedia programs in which contractual obligations with vendors are stated to include ISD components such as learner analysis, design limitations, development plans, delivery, and methods of learner evaluation.

The ISD model is a theoretic, offering a generic framework with established tasks for the instructional designer to perform in preparing training programs. However, the procedures specified to complete each stage of a training program's development were based on psychological principles derived mainly from behaviorism and are being updated with recent advances in cognitive science.

Opting for the potential cost-effectiveness of newer, more technological modes of presentation may not necessarily provide for all student or training system needs. More likely is a scenario in which new methods supplement proven approaches to transfer, such as ISD. A fair conclusion can be made: Basics still apply and should be accomplished to maximize performance competency in those being trained. What follows is a quick review of the essential components of the basic ISD model.

Analyze, Design, Develop, Implement, Evaluate (ADDIE)

Analyze

This phase requires that the trainer first become familiar with every aspect of the operational system, job, or educational situation for which there is thought to be a need for instruction: Do we need to teach something? What is the subject all about? What should the learner be able to do? (Figure 4.8)

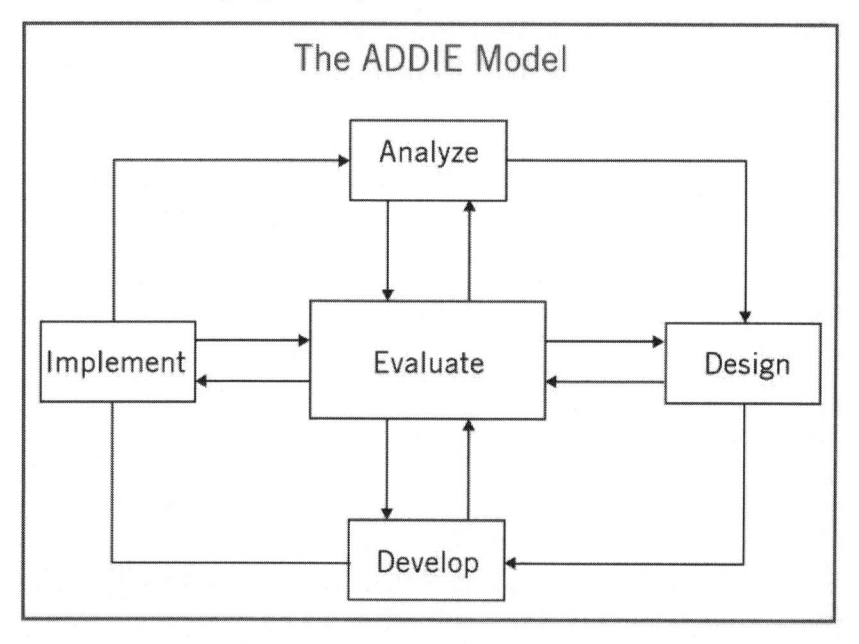

Figure 4.8 ADDIE Model

Analysis will help determine whether there is a need for instruction, what will be taught, and what behaviors and processes the learner should exhibit. This part of the process is dedicated to the collection of data, which should be used to determine the purpose of the operational system, job, or educational situation to be taught, including the following elements:

- Functional responsibilities of personnel working within the operational system, job, or educational situation to be taught.
- Operational subsystems structure or knowledge base to be taught.
- Support equipment or materials.
- How information about the system or educational situation is maintained or used.

The products of analysis should include:

- The basic human physical and mental processes required.
- A list of all job tasks and procedures.
- The equipment and materials involved in each task.
- The conditions under which the task must be done.
- The performance standards (degree of competency) to be demonstrated.
- In the final phases of analysis a developer should determine.
- How often a task needs to be accomplished.
- Task criticality.
- Task complexity.
- Difficulty level required to learn and teach each task.

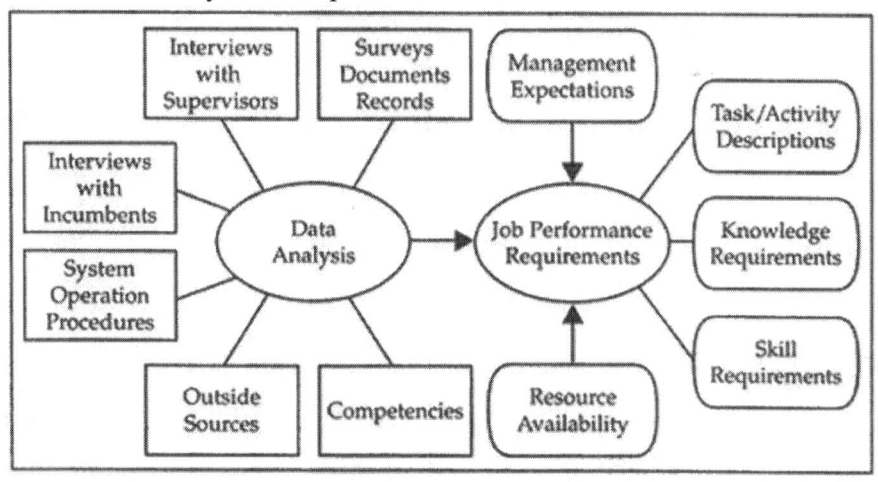

Figure 4.9 Typical Flowchart of Analysis-to-Design Phase Design

Once the job performance requirements are known, the trainer must determine the difference between the skills possessed by those targeted for training and the skills required to operate the system or master the educational challenge. The resulting data constitute the training or education requirements. The trainer will use the initial data to build the course design by considering the following:

- What training is needed most
- Criticality of tasks and knowledge
- Frequency of performance
- Complexity of tasks
- Difficulty of learning
- Time interval between initial training and initial performance
- Availability of time, instructors, equipment, facilities, and funding

Develop

This is the phase when inexperience can lead to the selection of inappropriate materials from vendors. For example, a "generic" problem-solving video may not provide the appropriate context unless special "customization" is included. Another example is using an off-the-shelf time-management program for call center supervisors. Anybody who has visited or works in a call center will know what it means when we say "context, context, context."

One of the purported limitations of ISD is that it originally was based on behaviorism and that not until recently was cognitive science introduced to provide a more robust approach to developing the knowledge, skills, and attitudes that result in the desired human performance. Through understanding and experimenting with recent developments in cognitive science, trainers have been able to enhance procedural (behavior-based) as well as mental skills by applying unique and creative designs to training.

Implement

Depending on the size of the training effort, the following implementation plan requirements need to be situated in this phase of the ISD process. Actually, many of these requirements need to be identified in the analysis phase to provide the resources necessary for successful implementation.

An implementation plan, also called a master training plan, should include the following:

- Administrative details.
- Audience to be trained (demographics).
- Schedules and venue (logistics).
- Curriculum path, map, and modules.
- Test and evaluation procedures.
- Trainers assigned.
- Budget.

Other support factors to be considered prior to training include:

- Trainer competencies.
- Records and reports (systems).
- Regulatory and legal considerations.
- Overall project management.

The actual conduct of the training should make most of the no instructional aspects of implementation transparent to the learner.

Evaluation

Ensure that evaluation instruments are in place that measure both instruction and how well the students do. Measurement takes many forms, however. As was stated in the development step, measurement devices must evaluate both supporting knowledge and the behavior of the objective under the conditions and subject to the standards as they are stated in the objective. The best instructional systems take the student through an experience that mirrors the work environment and maximizes student activities that are identical to job functions.

This fifth or final phase of ISD evaluation consists of two major activities:
1. *Internal evaluation* basically provides inputs based on the experience of trainers, staff, and learners that measure points of quality, including learner knowledge and performance checks. The overall purpose is to provide immediate or nearly immediate feedback to the instructional developers so that changes and / or modifications can be made to the curriculum. This is where "formative evaluation" applies.
2. *External evaluation* is directed fundamentally to application on the job; it includes Kirkpatrick's four levels as well as Parry's return on investment (ROI).This is where "summative evaluation" techniques apply; it is also where instructional objectives can be demonstrated through changes in human performance.

Chapter 12: Evaluating Training Programs

Some training and development professionals believe that evaluation means measuring changes in behavior that occur as a result of training programs. Others maintain that evaluation lies in determining the final results that have occurred because of training programs. Still others think only in terms of the comment sheets that participants complete at the end of a program. Still others are concerned with the learning that takes place in the classroom, as measured by increased knowledge, improved skills, and changes in attitude. They are all right and wrong, because they fail to recognize that all four approaches are parts of what is meant by evaluating. And that is according to Kirkpatrick evaluation levels.

Kirkpatrick developed a four level evaluation method that is in my personal opinion the most effective and accurate method.

The four levels represent a sequence of ways to evaluate programs. Each level is important. As one moves from one level to the next, the process becomes more difficult and time-consuming but also provides more valuable information.

None of the levels should be bypassed simply to get to the level the trainer considers the most important. The four levels are

Level 1: reaction
Level 2: learning
Level 3: behavior
Level 4: results

Level 1
Reaction

This level measures how your trainees (the people being trained), reacted to the training. Obviously, you want them to feel that the training was a valuable experience, and you want them to feel good about the instructor, the topic, the material, its presentation, and the venue.

It's important to measure reaction; because it helps you understand how well the training was received by your audience. It also helps you improve the training for future trainees, including identifying important areas or topics that are missing from the training.

Ok all that sounds textbook great, but are there any guidelines to go on? Yes they are:

1. Determine what you want to find out.
2. Design a form that will quantify reactions.
3. Encourage written comments and suggestions.
4. Get a 100 percent immediate response.
5. Get honest responses.
6. Develop acceptable standards.
7. Measure reactions against standards and take the appropriate action.
8. Communicate reactions as appropriate.

Level 2
Learning

At level 2, you measure what your trainees have learned. How much has their knowledge increased as a result of the training?

When you planned the training session, you hopefully started with a list of specific learning objectives: these should be the starting point for your measurement. Keep in mind that you can measure learning in different ways depending on these objectives, and depending on whether you're interested in changes to knowledge, skills, or attitude.

It's important to measure this, because knowing what your trainees are learning and what they aren't will help you improve future training.

Guidelines for Evaluating Learning:

1. Use a control group if that is practical.
2. Evaluate knowledge, skills, and / or attitudes both before and after the program. Use a paper-and-pencil test to measure knowledge and attitudes and use a performance test to measure skills. Employ E-mail if you have the capability.
3. Get a 100 percent response.
4. Use the results of the evaluation to take appropriate action.

Level 3
Behavior

At this level, you evaluate how far your trainees have changed their behavior, based on the training they received. Specifically, this looks at how trainees apply the information.

Suppose no change in behavior is discovered. The obvious conclusion is that the program was ineffective and should be discontinued. This conclusion may or may not be accurate. The reaction may have been favorable and the learning objectives may have been accomplished, but the level 3 or level 4 conditions may not have been present. For change to occur, four conditions are necessary:

- The person must have a desire to change.
- The person must know what to do and how to do it.
- The person must work in the right climate.
- The person must be rewarded for changing.

The training program can accomplish the first two requirements by creating a positive attitude toward the desired change and teaching the necessary knowledge and skills. The third condition he right climate refers to the participant's immediate supervisor. Five different kinds of climate can be described:

- ➤ *Preventing.* The boss forbids the participant from doing what he or she has been taught to do in the training program. The boss may be influenced by the organizational culture established by top management, or the boss's leadership style may conflict with what was taught.
- ➤ *Discouraging.* The boss doesn't say, "You can't do it," but he or she makes it clear that the participant should not change his or her behavior because that would make the boss unhappy. Or the boss may not model the behavior taught in the program, and this negative example discourages the subordinate from changing.
- ➤ *Neutral.* The boss ignores the fact that the participant has attended a training program. It is business as usual. If the subordinate wants to change, the boss has no objection as long as the job gets done. If negative results occur because behavior has changed, the boss may create a discouraging or even preventing climate.
- ➤ *Encouraging.* The boss encourages the participant to learn and to apply his or her learning on the job. Ideally, the boss discussed the program with the subordinate beforehand and stated that they would discuss its application as soon as the program was over. The boss basically says, "I am interested in knowing what you learned and how I can help you transfer the learning to the job."
- ➤ *Requiring.* The boss knows what the subordinate learns and makes sure the learning transfers to the job. In some cases a learning contract is prepared that states what the subordinate agrees to do. This contract can be prepared at the end of the training session, and a copy can be given to the boss. The boss sees to it that the contract is implemented.

Guidelines for Evaluating Behavior:

1. Use a control group if that is practical.
2. Allow time for a change in behavior to take place.
3. Evaluate both before and after the program if that is practical.

4. Survey and / or interview one or more of the following: trainees, their immediate supervisors, their subordinates, and others who often observe their behavior.
5. Get a 100 percent response.
6. Repeat the evaluation at appropriate times.
7. Consider cost versus benefits.

Level 4
Results

Results can be defined as the final results that occurred because the participants attended the program. The final results can include increased production, improved quality, decreased costs, reduced frequency and/or severity of accidents, increased sales, reduced turnover, and higher profits and return on investment. It is important to recognize that results like these are the reason for having some training programs. Therefore, the final objectives of the training program must be stated in these terms.

Some programs have these things in mind on what can be called a far-out basis. For example, one major objective of the popular program on diversity in the work force is to change the attitudes of supervisors and managers toward minority group members in their departments. We want supervisors to treat all people fairly, show no discrimination, and so on. These are not tangible results that can be measured in terms of dollars and cents, but it is hoped that tangible results will follow. Similarly, it is difficult if not impossible to measure final results for programs on topics such as leadership, communication, motivation, time management, empowerment, decision making, and managing change. We can state and evaluate desired behaviors, but the final results have to be measured in terms of improved morale or other nonfinancial terms. It is hoped that things such as higher morale and improved quality of work life will result in the tangible results just described.

Guidelines for Evaluating Results:

1. Use a control group if that is practical.
2. Allow time for results to be achieved.
3. Measure both before and after the program if that is practical.
4. Repeat the measurement at appropriate times.
5. Consider cost versus benefits.
6. Be satisfied with evidence if proof is not possible.

Evaluating results (level 4) provides the greatest challenge to training professionals. After all, that is why we train, and we ought to be able to show tangible results that more than pay for the cost of training. In some cases such evaluation can be done easily. Programs that aim at increasing sales and reducing accidents, turnover, and scrap rates often can be evaluated in terms of results, and the cost of a program isn't too difficult to determine. A comparison can readily show that training pays off.

Chapter 13: Measuring the Return on Investment

Measuring the return on investment (ROI) in training and development and performance improvement has consistently earned a place among the critical issues in the Human Resource Development (HRD) field. The topic appears routinely on conference agendas and at professional meetings. Journals and newsletters regularly embrace the concept with increasing print space. A professional organization has been developed to exchange information on ROI. At least a dozen books provide significant coverage of the topic. Even top executives have stepped up their appetite for ROI information.

Measuring ROI is a topic of much debate. It is rare for any topic to stir up emotions to the degree the ROI issue does. Return on investment is characterized as flawed and inappropriate by some, while others describe it as the only answer to their accountability concerns. The truth probably lies somewhere in between. Understanding the drivers for the ROI process and the inherent weaknesses and advantages of ROI makes it possible to take a rational approach to the issue and implement an appropriate mix of evaluation strategies that includes ROI. This chapter presents the basic issues and trends concerning ROI measurement.

Although the interest in the topic has heightened and much progress has been made, it is still an issue that challenges even the most sophisticated and progressive HRD departments. While some professionals argue that it is not possible to calculate the ROI, others quietly and deliberately proceed to develop measures and ROI calculations. The latter group is gaining tremendous support from the senior management team. Regardless of the position taken on the issue, the reasons for measuring the return still exist. Almost all HRD professionals share a concern that they must eventually show a return on their training investment; otherwise, training funds may be reduced or the HRD department may not be able to maintain or enhance its present status and influence in the organization.

The dilemma surrounding the ROI process is a source of frustration with many senior executives even within the HRD field itself. Most executives realize that training is a basic necessity when organizations are experiencing significant growth or increased competition. In those cases, training can provide employees with the required skills while fine-tuning skills needed to meet competitive challenges. Training is also important during business restructuring and rapid change where employees must learn new skills and often find themselves doing much more work in a dramatically downsized workforce.

Most executives recognize the need for training and intuitively feel that there is value in training. They can logically conclude that training can pay off in important bottom-line measures such as productivity improvements, quality enhancements, cost reductions, and time savings. They also believe that training can enhance customer satisfaction, improve morale, and build teamwork. Yet, the frustration comes from the lack of evidence to show that the process is really working. While the payoffs are assumed to exist and training appears to be needed, more evidence is needed, or training funds may not be allocated in the future. The ROI methodology represents the most promising way to show this accountability in a logical, rational approach.

ROI Progress and Status

Before examining the progress of ROI, a few global trends about measurement and evaluation in both private and public sector organizations should be examined. The following measurement trends have been identified in our research and are slowly evolving across organizations and cultures in more than 35 countries (Phillips and Guadet, 2003). Collectively, these eleven important trends have significant impact on the way accountability is addressed:

- Evaluation is an integral part of the design, development, delivery, and implementation of programs.
- A shift from a reactive approach to a more proactive approach is developing, with evaluation addressed early in the cycle.
- Measurement and evaluation processes are systematic and methodical, often built into the delivery process.

- Technology is significantly enhancing the measurement and evaluation process, enabling large amounts of data to be collected, processed, analyzed, and integrated across programs.
- Evaluation planning is becoming a critical part of the measurement and evaluation cycle.
- The implementation of a comprehensive measurement and evaluation process usually leads to increased emphasis on the initial needs analysis.
- Organizations without comprehensive measurement and evaluation have reduced or eliminated their program budgets.
- Organizations with comprehensive measurement and evaluation have enhanced their program budgets.
- The use of ROI is emerging as an essential part of the measurement and evaluation mix.
- Many successful examples of comprehensive measurement and evaluation applications are available.
- A comprehensive measurement and evaluation process, including ROI, can be implemented for about 4 or 5% of the direct program budget.

The ROI methodology described in this book had its beginnings in the 1970s when it was applied to the development of a return on investment for a supervisory training program. Since then it has been developed, modified, and refined to represent the process reported here and expanded in all types of situations, applications, and sectors. Figure 5.0 shows how the process has evolved within the different sectors. Applications began in the manufacturing sector, where the process is easily developed. It migrated to the service sector, as major service firms such as banks and telecommunications companies used the ROI process to show the value of various programs. Applications evolved into the health care arena as the industry sought ways to improve educational services, human resources, quality, risk management, and case management. Nonprofit applications began to emerge as these organizations were seeking ways to reduce costs and generate efficiencies. Finally, applications in the public sector began to appear in a variety of types of government organizations. Public sector implementation has intensified in recent years. An outgrowth of public sector applications includes the use of the process in the educational field where it is now being applied in different settings. The implementation is spreading and all types of organizations and settings are now enjoying application of the ROI methodology.

Movement within the Sectors

Manufacturing Sector
↓
Service Sector
↓
Health Care Sector
↓
Nonprofit Sector
↓
Public Sector
↓
Educational Sector

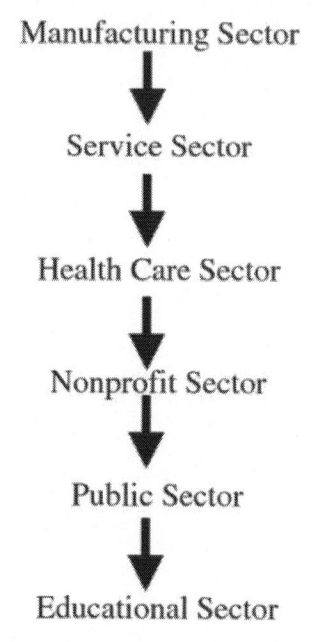

Figure 5.0 Progression of ROI implementation.

The specific types of program applications vary significantly. Table 1.0 shows a full range of current applications representing programs from training and development, education, human resources, change, and technology. Published cases exist in all of these areas. The process is flexible, versatile, and adaptable to almost any type of setting and environment.

ROI Applications

A Variety of Applications Are Possible

- Executive Education
- Leadership
- Executive Coaching
- Diversity Programs
- Wellness/Fitness Initiatives
- Total Quality Management
- Self-Directed Teams
- Skill-Based/Knowledge-Based Compensation
- Organization Development
- Retention Strategies
- Competency Systems
- Career Development Programs
- Recruiting Strategies
- Orientation Systems
- Associate Relations Programs
- Gainsharing Programs
- Technology Implementation
- Safety and Health Programs
- e-Learning

Table 1.0

The status of the ROI process among practitioners in the field is difficult to pinpoint. Senior HRD managers are reluctant to disclose internal practices and, even in the most progressive organizations, confess that too little progress has been made. Until recently, it was difficult to find cases in the literature that show how an organization has attempted to measure the return on investment in HRD. Recognizing this void as an opportunity, the American Society for Training and Development (ASTD) undertook an ambitious project to develop a collection of cases that represent real life examples of measuring the return on investment. To find cases, more than 2000 individuals were contacted for the initial volume, including practitioners, authors, researchers, consultants, and conference presenters. The response was very encouraging. Ultimately, 18 cases were selected for publication in Volume 1 of In Action: Measuring Return on Investment (Phillips, 1994). This publication has become the all-time best seller at ASTD from over 250 of the society's titles sold through catalogs, bookstores, and conferences. Because of the reaction and response, Volume 2 was developed and published three years later (Phillips, 1997). This volume has become the number 2 best seller. With that success, and continuing demand, Volume 3 was published four years later (Phillips, 2001).

The various studies indicate the use of, and interest in, the ROI method- ology continue to show promise. For example, the American Society for Training and Development (ASTD) concluded in the 2002 industry report that the number one global trend and issue facing human resource development practitioners is developing the return on investment in training (Van Buren, 2002). The trend and issue was number two the year before, underscoring its continuing dominance of the issue, but a growing trend as well.

Research studies are continuously conducted to show the progress of ROI as well as the dilemmas concerning ROI. Perhaps one of the most comprehensive studies was conducted by the Corporate Leadership Council involving 278 organizations showing the tremendous interest in ROI (Drimmer, 2002). This study attempted to understand the variety of metrics desired and utilized by training and development practitioners. Although several metrics were explored, Table 1-1 shows the status of ROI and business impact as training and development metrics. As the table shows, 78% of the organizations have ROI on their wish list, rating it either important or very important as a desired metric. However, those same organizations currently indicate that 11% of them are using ROI. The same comparison is presented for ROI in development (which are the non-training types of programs) as well as the business impact measure (where the impact of training experiences on performance is developed). Two important issues evolve from this study. First, the use of ROI continues to grow. A total of 13% of organizations are using ROI in training and development. This is up from previous reports of utilization. Second, there is tremendous interest in ROI, showing that almost 80% of the organizations are pursuing it. This creates a significant dilemma for organizations and underscores the lack of understanding for ROI, the misconceptions of the methodology, and the difficulty in making it work in certain situations. Nevertheless, it out- lines a tremendous opportunity (instead of problem) as organizations strive to bring more accountability through the use of the ROI methodology.

ROI Opportunies

Metric	Percentage of organizations rating metric as important or very important (wish list)	Percentage of organizations indicating utilization of metric (doing list)
ROI in Training	78%	11%
ROI in Development	62%	2%
Impact of Training Experiences on Performance	88%	27%

Table 1.1

Another major study attempted to determine how organizations measure the impact of corporate universities (Phillips, 2000). A detailed benchmarking study examined how major corporate universities are dealing with the accountability issue and, in particular, ROI. Among the conclusions are that best-practice corporate universities are moving up the levels of evaluation, up to and including business impact and ROI. These same corporate universities also want to use ROI, but are struggling with how to calculate it and what to do with the results. These and other studies indicate two important conclusions.

1. There is a tremendous and growing interest in the ROI method- ology as a training and development evaluation tool all around the globe.
2. While progress has been made, there is much more progress to be made to reach the desired level of utilization.

Perhaps one of the most visible signs of the acceptance of ROI method- ology is the ASTD ROI Network. Founded in 1996, the ROI Network was formed by a group of practitioners involved in implementing the ROI process. The purpose of the organization is to promote the science and practice of individual and organizational measurement and accountability. The network established three strategic goals:

1. To leverage the knowledge, skills, and experience of practitioners and sponsors.

2. To reinforce and support practitioner knowledge, skills, and experience.
3. To promote innovative ROI measurement and evaluation practices.

Through websites, list servers, newsletters, research grants, and conferences, the network has routinely exchanged information around the ROI process. Membership is global as are the ROI Network board members. In 2002, the network was acquired by the American Society for Training and Development and now operates as the ASTD ROI Network, initially with 400 members. Membership in the network is an option available to all ASTD members under one of its classic member- ship options (www.ASTD.org).

Measuring the return on investment is becoming a truly global issue. Organizations from all over the world are concerned about the account- ability of training and are exploring ways and techniques to measure the results of training. In a survey of 35 members of the International Federation of Training and Development Organizations, measuring return on investment was consistently rated the hottest topic among members of those organizations (Phillips, 1999). Whether the economy is mature or developing, the accountability of training is still a critical issue. Many professional associations in different countries have offered workshops, seminars, and dedicated conferences to the measurement issue, including ROI. Some associations have sponsored individual workshops on ROI. The formal ROI presentations have been made in over 50 countries with implementation organized and coordinated in at least 35 countries. Two examples underscore the role of these organizations in implementing ROI in their respective countries. Enterprise Ireland, an Ireland government agency, sponsored workshops on ROI for training and development professionals, followed by workshops for executives. The agency took the lead in coordinating and introducing ROI to organizations in Ireland.

Japan Management Association (JMA), an organization of medium to large business organizations in Japan, introduced the ROI process to its member organizations. JMA translated one of the major books on ROI and sponsored workshops and other learning activities around the ROI process. JMA is coordinating the implementation of the ROI methodology in Japan.

The progress with ROI underscores the need for training and performance improvement to shift from an activity-based process to a results based process. As depicted in Table 1-2, a significant paradigm shift has occurred in recent years that will have a dramatic effect on the account- ability of training, education, and development programs. Organizations have moved from training for activity to training with a focus on bottom-line results, and this shift is evident from the beginning to the end of the process.

Paradigm Shift in Training and Performance Improvement

Activity Based	Results Based
Characterized by:	Characterized by:
☐ no business need for the program	☐ program linked to specific business needs
☐ no assessment of performance issues	☐ assessment of performance effectiveness
☐ no specific measurable objectives for application and impact	☐ specific objectives for application and impact
☐ no effort to prepare program participants to achieve results	☐ results expectations communicated to participants
☐ no effort to prepare the work environment to support application	☐ environment prepared to support transfer of learning
☐ no efforts to build partnerships with key managers	☐ partnerships established with key managers and clients
☐ no measurement of results or cost benefit analysis	☐ measurement of results and cost benefit analysis
☐ planning and reporting is input-focused	☐ planning and reporting is output-focused

One thing is certain in the ROI debate—it is not a fad. As long as there is a need for accountability of training expenditures and the concept of an investment payoff is desired, ROI will be utilized to evaluate major investments in training and performance improvement. A "fad" is a new idea or approach or a new spin on an old approach. The concept of ROI has been used for centuries. The 75th anniversary issue of Harvard Business Review (HBR) traced the tools used to measure results in organizations (Sibbet, 1997). In the early issues of HBR, during the 1920s, ROI was the emerging tool to place a value on the payoff of investments. With increased adoption and use, it appears that ROI is here to stay. Today, hundreds of organizations are routinely developing ROI calculations for training and performance improvement programs. Its status has grown significantly and the rate of implementation has been phenomenal. The number of organizations and individuals involved with the process underscores the magnitude of ROI implementation. Table 1-4 presents a summary of the current status. With this much evidence of the growing interest, the ROI process is now becoming a standard tool for program evaluation.

Why ROI?

There are good reasons why return on investment has gained acceptance. Although the viewpoints and explanations may vary, some things are very clear. The key issues are outlined here.

- The ROI methodology has been refined over a 25-year period.
- The ROI methodology has been adopted by hundreds of organizations in manufacturing, service, nonprofit, and government settings.
- Thousands of studies are developed each year using the ROI methodology.
- A hundred case studies are published on the ROI methodology.
- Two thousand individuals have been certified to implement the ROI methodology in their organizations.
- Organizations in 35 countries have implemented the ROI methodology.
- Fourteen books have been developed to support the process
- A 400-member professional network has been formed to share information.
- The ROI methodology can be implemented for 4–5% of the HRD budget.

The ROI process adds a fifth level to the four levels of evaluation, which were developed almost 40 years ago (Kirkpatrick, 1975).

At Level 5, Return on Investment (the ultimate level of evaluation), the measurement compares the program's monetary benefits with the program costs. The evaluation cycle is not complete until the Level 5 evaluation is conducted.

ROI applications have increased because of the growing interest in a variety of organizational improvement, quality, and change programs, which have dominated in organizations, particularly in North America, Europe, and Asia. Organizations have embraced almost any trend or fad that has appeared on the horizon. Unfortunately, many of these change efforts have not been successful and have turned out to be passing fads embraced in attempts to improve the organizations. The training and development function is often caught in the middle of this activity, either by supporting the process with programs or actually coordinating the new process in these organizations. While the ROI process is an effective way to measure the accountability of training, it has rarely been used in the past. A complete implementation of the process requires thorough needs assessment and significant planning before an ROI program is implemented. If these two elements are in place, unnecessary passing fads, doomed for failure, can be avoided. With the ROI process in place, a new change program that does not produce results will be exposed. Management will be aware of it early so that adjustments can be made.

Total Quality Management, Continuous Process Improvement, and Six Sigma have brought increased attention to measurement issues. Today, organizations measure processes and outputs that were not previously measured, monitored, and reported. This focus has placed increased pressure on the training and development function to develop measures of program success. Restructuring and reengineering initiatives and the threat of out- sourcing have caused training executives to focus more directly on bottom-line issues. Many training processes have been reengineered to align programs more closely with business needs, and obtain maximum efficiencies in the training cycle. These change processes have brought increased attention to evaluation issues and have resulted in measuring the contribution of specific programs, including ROI.

The business management mindset of many current education and training managers causes them to place more emphasis on economic issues within the function. Today's education and training manager is more aware of bottom-line issues in the organization and more knowledgeable of operational and financial concerns. This new "enlightened" manager often takes a business approach to training and development, with ROI as part of the strategy (Van Adelsberg and Trolley, 1999). ROI is a familiar term and concept for business managers, particularly those with business administration and management degrees. They have studied the ROI process in their academic preparation where ROI is to evaluate the purchase of equipment, building a new facility, or buying a new company. Consequently, they understand and appreciate ROI and are pleased to see the ROI methodology applied to the evaluation of training and performance improvement.

ROI is now taking on increased interest in the executive suite. Top executives who watched their training budgets continue to grow without the appropriate accountability measures have become frustrated and, in an attempt to respond to the situation, have turned to ROI. Top executives are now demanding return on investment calculations from departments and functions where they were not previously required. For years, training and development managers convinced top executives that training couldn't be measured, at least at the monetary contribution level. Yet, many of the executives are now aware that it can and is being measured in many organizations. Top executives are subsequently demanding the same accountability from their training and development functions.

The Concerns with ROI

Although much progress has been made, the ROI process is not without its share of problems and concerns. The mere presence of the process creates a dilemma for many organizations. When an organization embraces the concept and implements the process, the management team is usually anxiously waiting for results, only to be disappointed when they are not readily available. For an ROI process to be useful, it must balance many issues such as feasibility, simplicity, credibility, and sound- ness. More specifically, three major audiences must be pleased with the ROI process to accept and use it:

- Practitioners who design, develop, and delivery programs.
- Senior managers, sponsors, and clients who initiate and support programs.
- Researchers who need a credible process.

For years, HRD practitioners have assumed that ROI could not be measured. When they examined a typical process, they found long formulas, complicated equations, and complex models that made the ROI process appear too confusing. With this perceived complexity, HRD managers could visualize the tremendous efforts required for data col- lection and analysis, and more importantly, the increased cost necessary to make the process work. Because of these concerns, HRD practitioners are seeking an ROI process that is simple and easy to understand so that they can easily implement the steps and strategies. They also need a process that will not take an excessive time frame to implement and will not consume too much precious staff time. Finally, practitioners need a process that is not too expensive. With competition for financial resources, they need a process that will require only a small portion of the HRD budget. In summary, the ROI process, from the perspective of the HRD practitioner, must be user friendly, save time, and be cost efficient.

Criteria for an Effective ROI Process

To satisfy the needs of the three critical groups described above, the ROI process must meet several requirements. Eleven essential criteria for an effective ROI process follow:

1. The ROI process must be simple, void of complex formulas, lengthy equations, and complicated methodologies. Most ROI attempts have failed with this requirement. In an attempt to obtain statistical perfection and use too many theories, some ROI models have become too complex to understand and use. Consequently, they have not been implemented.
2. The ROI process must be economical and must be implemented easily. The process should become a routine part of training and development without requiring significant additional resources. Sampling for ROI calcu-

lations and early planning for ROI are often necessary to make progress without adding new staff.

3. The assumptions, methodology, and techniques must be <u>credible</u>. Logical, methodical steps are needed to earn the respect of practitioners, senior managers, and researchers. This requires a very practical approach for the process.

4. From a research perspective, the ROI process must be <u>theoretically sound</u> and based on generally accepted practices. Unfortunately, this requirement can lead to an extensive, complicated process. Ideally, the process must strike a balance between maintaining a practical and sensible approach and a sound and theoretical basis for the process. This is perhaps one of the greatest challenges to those who have developed models for the ROI process.

5. The ROI process must <u>account for other factors</u> that have influenced output variables. One of the most often overlooked issues, isolating the influence of the HRD program, is necessary to build credibility and accuracy within the process. The ROI process should pinpoint the contribution of the training program when compared to the other influences.

6. The ROI process must be appropriate with a <u>variety of HRD programs</u>. Some models apply to only a small number of programs such as sales or productivity training. Ideally, the process must be applicable to all types of training and other HRD programs such as career development, organization development, and major change initiatives.

7. The ROI process must have the <u>flexibility</u> to be applied on a pre- program basis as well as a post program basis. In some situations, an estimate of the ROI is required before the actual program is developed. Ideally, the process should be able to adjust to a range of potential time frames.

8. The ROI process must be applicable with all types of data, including hard data, which are typically represented as output, quality, costs, and time; and soft data, which include job satisfaction, customer satisfaction, absenteeism, turnover, grievances, and complaints.

9. The ROI process must include the costs of the program. The ultimate level of evaluation is to compare the benefits with costs. Although the term ROI has been loosely used to express any benefit of training, an acceptable ROI formula must include costs. Omitting or underestimating costs will only destroy the credibility of the ROI values.
10. The actual calculation must use an acceptable ROI formula. This is often the benefits/cost ratio (BCR) or the ROI calculation, expressed as a percent. These formulas compare the actual expenditure for the program with the monetary benefits driven from the program. While other financial terms can be substituted, it is important to use a standard financial calculation in the ROI process.
11. Finally, the ROI process must have a successful track record in a variety of applications. In far too many situations, models are created but never successfully applied. An effective ROI process should withstand the wear and tear of implementation and should get the results expected.

Because these criteria are considered essential, an ROI methodology should meet the vast majority, if not all criteria. The bad news is that most ROI processes do not meet these criteria.

A final definition offered in this chapter is the basic definition of return on investment. Two common formulas are offered: Benefits/Costs Ratio (BCR) and ROI:

$$BCR = \frac{\text{Program Benefits}}{\text{Program Costs}}$$

$$ROI\ (\%) = \frac{\text{Net Program Benefits}}{\text{Program Costs}} \times 100$$

The BCR uses the total benefits and costs. In the ROI formula, the costs are subtracted from the total benefits to produce net benefits which are then divided by the costs. For example, a telemarketing sales training program at Hewlett-Packard Company produced benefits of $3,296,977 with a cost of $1,116,291 (Seagraves, 2001). Therefore, the benefits/costs ratio is:

$$BCR = \frac{\$3,296,977}{\$1,116,291} = 2.95 \text{ (or 2.95:1)}$$

As this calculation shows, for every $1 invested, $2.95 in benefits are returned. In this example, net benefits are $3,296,977 - $1,116,291 = $2,180,616. Thus, the ROI is:

$$ROI (\%) = \frac{\$2,180,616}{\$1,116,291} \times 100 = 195\%$$

This means that for each $1 invested in the program, there is a return of $1.95 in net benefits, after costs are covered. The benefits are usually expressed as annual benefits, representing the amount saved or gained for a complete year after program completion. While the benefits may continue after the first year if the program has long-term effects, the impact usually diminishes and is omitted from calculations. This conservative approach is used throughout the application of the ROI process in this book. The values for return on investment are usually quite large, in the range of 25 to 500%, which illustrates the potential impact of successful programs.

Barriers to ROI Implementation

Costs and Time

The ROI process will add some additional costs and time to the evaluation process of programs, although the added amount will not be excessive. It is possible this barrier alone stops many ROI implementations early in the process. A comprehensive ROI process can be implemented for 3–5% to the overall training budget. The additional investment in ROI could perhaps be offset by the additional results achieved from these programs and the elimination of unproductive or unprofitable programs.

Lack of Skills and Orientation for HRD Staff

Many training and performance improvement staff members do not understand ROI nor do they have the basic skills necessary to apply the process within their scope of responsibilities. Measurement and evaluation is not usually part of the preparation for the job. Also, the typical training program does not focus on results, but more on learning out- comes. Staff members attempt to measure results by measuring learning. Consequently, a tremendous barrier to implementation is the change needed for the overall orientation, attitude, and skills of the HRD staff.

Faulty Needs Assessment

Many of the current HRD programs do not have an adequate needs assessment. Some of these programs have been implemented for the wrong reasons based on management requests or efforts to chase a popular fad or trend in the industry. If the program is not needed, the benefits from the program will be minimal. An ROI calculation for an unnecessary program will likely yield a negative value. This is a realistic barrier for many programs.

Fear

Some HRD departments do not pursue ROI because of fear of failure or fear of the unknown. Fear of failure appears in many ways. Designers, developers, facilitators, and program owners may be concerned about the consequence of negative ROI. They fear that ROI will be a performance evaluation tool instead of a process improvement tool. The ROI process will also stir up the traditional fear of change. This fear, often based on unrealistic assumptions and a lack of knowledge of the process, becomes a realistic barrier to many ROI implementations.

Discipline and Planning

A successful ROI implementation requires much planning and a disciplined approach to keep the process on track. Implementation schedules, evaluation targets, ROI analysis plans, measurement and evaluation policies, and follow-up schedules are required. The HRD staff may not have enough discipline and determination to stay on course. This becomes a barrier, particularly when there are no immediate pressures to measure the return. If the current senior management group is not requiring ROI, the HRD staff may not allocate time for planning and coordination. Other pressures and priorities also often eat into the time necessary for ROI implementation. Only carefully planned implementation will be successful.

False Assumptions

Many HRD staff members have false assumptions about the ROI process that keep them from attempting ROI. Typical of these assumptions are the following:

- The impact of a training program cannot be accurately calculated.
- Managers do not want to see the results of training and development expressed in monetary values.
- If the CEO does not ask for the ROI, he or she is not expecting it.
- "I have a professional, competent staff. Therefore, I do not have to justify the effectiveness of our programs."
- The training process is a complex, but necessary activity. There- fore, it should not be subjected to an accountability process.

Benefits of ROI

Although the benefits of adopting the ROI process may appear to be obvious, several distinct and important benefits can be derived from the implementation of ROI in an organization. These key benefits, inherent with almost any type of impact evaluation process, make the ROI process an attractive challenge for the human resource development function.

Measure Contribution

It is the most accurate, credible, and widely used process to show the impact of training. The HRD staff will know the specific contribution from a select number of programs. The ROI will determine if the benefits of the program, expressed in monetary values, have outweighed the costs. It will determine if the program made a contribution to the organization and if it was, indeed, a good investment.

Set Priorities

Calculating ROI in different areas will determine which programs con- tribute the most to the organization, allowing priorities to be established for high impact training. Successful programs can be expanded into other areas if the same need is there ahead of other programs. Inefficient programs can be designed and redeployed. Ineffective programs may be discontinued.

Focus on Results

The ROI process is a results-based process that brings a focus on results with all programs, even for those not targeted for an ROI calculation. The process requires instructional designers, facilitators, participants, and support groups to concentrate on measurable objectives: what the program is attempting to accomplish. Thus, this process has the added benefit of improving the effectiveness of all training programs.

Alter Management Perceptions of Training

The ROI process, when applied consistently and comprehensively, can convince the management group that training is an investment and not an expense. Managers will see training as making a viable contribution to their objectives, thus increasing the respect for the function. This is an important step in building a partnership with management and increasing management support for training.

ROI Best Practices

The continuing progress with ROI implementation has provided an opportunity to determine if specific strategies are common among organizations pursuing the ROI process. Several common strategies that are considered to be the best practices for measurement and evaluation have emerged. Whether they meet the test to be labeled "best practice" will never be known, since it is risky to label any practice as a best practice. Although the following strategies are presented as a comprehensive framework, few organizations have adopted all of them.

It is difficult to evaluate an entire HRD function such as management development, career development, executive education, or technical training. The ROI process is more effective when applied to one program that can be linked to a direct payoff. In situations where a series of courses with common objectives must be completed before the objectives can be met, an evaluation of the series of courses may be appropriate. For this reason, ROI evaluation should be considered as a micro-level activity that will usually focus on a single program or a few tightly integrated programs. This decision to evaluate several pro- grams—or just one program—should include consideration of objectives of the program, timing of the programs, and cohesiveness of the series. Attempting to evaluate a group of programs conducted over a long period becomes quite difficult. The cause and effect relationship becomes more confusing and complex.

Best practice companies use a variety of approaches to collect evaluation data. They do not become aligned with one or two practices that dominate data collection, regardless of the situation. They recognize that each program, setting, and situation is different and, consequently, different techniques are needed to collect the data. Interviews, focus groups, and questionnaires work quite well in some situations. In others, action plans, performance contracts, and performance monitoring are needed to determine the specific impact of the program. These organizations deliberately match the data collection method with the program, following a set of criteria developed internally.

One of the most critical elements of the ROI process is attempting to isolate the impact of the training program from other influences that may have occurred during the same time period. Best practice organizations recognize that many influences affect business results measures. Although training is implemented in harmony with other systems and processes, sometimes there is a need to know the contribution of training, particularly when there are different process owners. Consequently, after a program is conducted, training must share only a part of the credit for improved performance. When an ROI calculation is planned, these organizations attempt to use one or more methods to isolate the effects of training. They go beyond the typical use of a control group arrangement, which has set the standard for this process for many years. They explore the use of a variety of other techniques to arrive at a realistic estimate of training's impact on output measures.

Because of the resources required for the process, most training pro- grams do not include ROI calculations. Therefore, organizations must determine the appropriate level of ROI evaluation. There is no pre- scribed formula, and the number of ROI impact studies depends on many variables, including:
- staff expertise on evaluation,
- the nature and type of HRD programs,
- resources that can be allocated to the process,
- the support from management for training and development,
- the organization's commitment to measurement and evaluation, and
- pressure from others to show ROI calculations.

Other variables specific to the organization may enter the process. It is rare for organizations to use statistical sampling when selecting sample programs that target ROI calculations. For most, this approach represents far too many calculations and too much analysis. Using a practical approach, most organizations settle on evaluating one or two sessions of their most popular programs. For example, Apple Computer developed an ROI calculation for their program, Process Improvement Teams (Burkett, 2001). Still others select a program from each of its major training segments. For example, in a large bank, with six academies, a program is selected each year from each academy for an ROI calculation. For organizations implementing the ROI concept for the first time, it is recommended that only one or two courses be selected for an initial calculation as a learning process. While it is important to be statistically sound in the approach to sapling, it is more important to consider a trade-off between resources available and the level of activity management is willing to accept for ROI calculations. The primary objective of an ROI calculation is not only to convince the HRD staff that the process works, but to show others (usually senior management) that HRD does make a difference. Therefore, it is important that the sampling plan be developed with the input and approval of senior management. In the final analysis, the selection process should yield a level of sampling in which senior management is comfortable in its accountability assessment of the HRD function.

Because the specific return on investment is needed, business impact data must be converted to monetary benefits. Best practice organizations are not content to show that a program improved productivity, enhanced quality, reduced employee turnover, decreased absenteeism, or increased customer satisfaction. They convert these data items to monetary units so that the benefits can be compared to costs, which in turn leads to an ROI calculation. These organizations take an extra step to develop a realistic value for these data items. For hard data items such as productivity, quality, and time, the process is relatively easy. However, for soft data items such as customer satisfaction, employee turnover, employee absenteeism, and job satisfaction, the process is more difficult. Yet, techniques are available, and are utilized, to make these conversions reasonably accurate.

Chapter 14: ROI Model

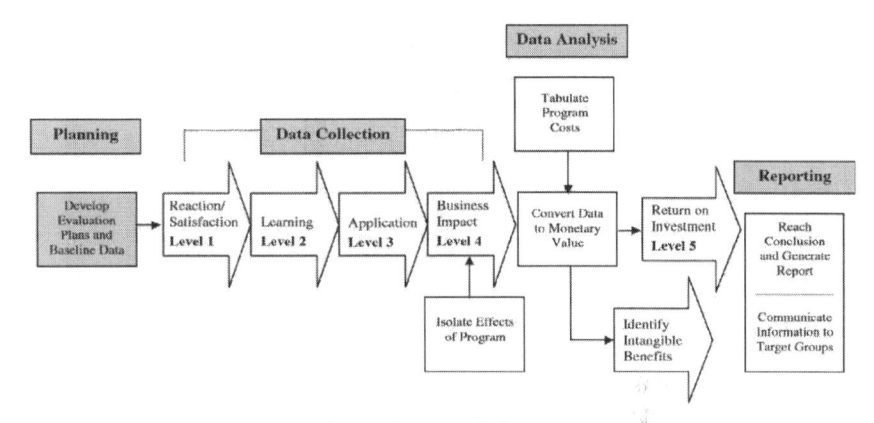

The ROI Module

The ROI model provides a systematic approach to ROI calculations. A step-by-step approach keeps the process manageable so that users can tackle one issue at a time. The model also emphasizes that this is a logical, systematic process that flows from one step to another. Applying the model provides consistency from one ROI calculation to another. Here we will describe the development of the complete ROI methodology and then briefly discusses each step of the model.

Building a comprehensive measurement and evaluation process is like a puzzle where the pieces are developed and put in place over time. Figure 5.1 depicts this puzzle and the pieces necessary to build a comprehensive measurement and evaluation process. The building block is the selection of an evaluation framework, which is a categorization of data. The balanced scorecard process (Kaplan and Norton, 1996) or the four levels of evaluation developed by Kirkpatrick (1975) offers the beginning point for such a framework. The framework selected for the process presented here is a modification of Kirkpatrick's four levels and includes a fifth level return on investment. A major building block, the ROI process model, is necessary to show how data are collected, processed, analyzed, and reported to various target audiences. This process model ensures that appropriate techniques and procedures are consistently used to address almost any situation. A third building block is the development of operating standards. These standards help ensure that the results of the study are stable and not influenced by the individual conducting the study. Replication is critical for the credibility of an evaluation process. The use of operating standards allows for replication, so that if more than one individual evaluates a specific program, the results are the same. In the ROI methodology, the operating standards are labeled as guiding principles.

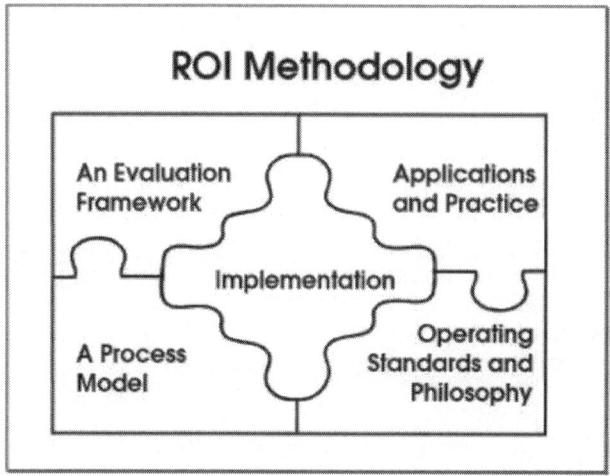

Figure 5.1 ROI methodology elements.

Next, appropriate attention must be given to implementation issues, as the ROI process becomes a routine part of training and performance. Several issues must be addressed involving skills, communication, roles, responsibilities, plans, and strategies. Finally, there must be successful applications and practice describing the implementation of the process within the organization, the value a comprehensive measurement and evaluation process brings to the organization, and the impact the specific program evaluated has on the organization.

The ROI Model

Reference to the ROI model presented at the beginning of this chapter, let's describe each item in the model.

Evaluation Planning

Several pieces of the evaluation puzzle must be explained when developing the evaluation plan for an ROI calculation. Three specific elements are important to evaluation success (purpose, feasibility, and objectives of programs) and are outlined in this section.

Although evaluation is usually undertaken to improve the HRD process, several distinct purposes can be identified. Evaluation is planned to:

- Improve the quality of learning and outcomes
- Determine whether a program is accomplishing its objectives
- Identify the strengths and weaknesses in the learning process
- Determine the benefits/costs analysis of an HRD program
- Assist in marketing HRD programs in the future
- Determine whether the program was appropriate for the target audience
- Establish a database, which can assist in making decisions about the programs
- Establish priorities for funding

Although there are other purposes of evaluation, these are some of the most important purposes (Russ-Eft and Preskill, 2001). Evaluation purposes should be considered prior to developing the evaluation plan because the purposes will often determine the scope of the evaluation, the types of instruments used, and the type of data collected. For example, when an ROI calculation is planned, one of the purposes would be to compare the costs and benefits of the program. This purpose has implications for the type of data collected (hard data), type of data col- lection method (performance monitoring), type of analysis (thorough), and the communication medium for results (formal evaluation report). For most programs, multiple evaluation purposes are pursued.

An important consideration in planning the ROI impact study is to deter- mine the appropriate levels for evaluation. Some evaluations will stop at Level 3, where a detailed report will determine the extent to which participants are using what they have learned. Others will be evaluated at Level 4, impact, where the consequences of their on-the-job application are monitored. A Level 4 impact study will examine hard and soft data measures directly linked to the program. This type of study will require that the impact of the program be isolated from other influences. Finally, if the ROI calculation is needed, two additional steps are required; the Level 4 impact data must be converted to monetary value and the costs of the program captured so that the ROI can be developed. Only a few programs should be taken to this level of evaluation. During the planning stage, the feasibility for a Level 4 or 5 impact study should be examined. Relevant questions that need to be addressed are:

- What specific measures have been influenced with this program?
- Are those measures readily available?
- Can the effect of the program on those measures be isolated?
- Are the costs of the program readily available?
- Will it be practical and feasible to discuss costs?
- Can the impact data be converted to monetary value?
- Is the actual ROI needed or necessary?

Training programs are evaluated at different levels as briefly described earlier. Corresponding to the levels of evaluation are levels of objectives:

- Reaction and Satisfaction objectives (1)
- Learning objectives (2)
- Application objectives (3)
- Impact objectives (4)
- ROI objectives (5)

Before the ROI evaluation begins, the program objectives must be identified or developed. The objectives form the basis for determining the depth of the evaluation, meaning that they determine what level of evaluation will take place. Historically, learning objectives are routinely developed. Application and impact objectives are not always in place, but are necessary for the proper focus on results.

Program objectives link directly to the front-end analysis. As shown in Figure 5.2, after the business need is determined (4), the needs analysis identifies the job performance (3) necessary to meet the business need. The skills and/or knowledge (2) needed to achieve the desired performance are identified, taking into consideration the preferences (1) for the learning solution to improve skills and knowledge. In the ROI method-ology, it is necessary to develop objectives at each level to ensure program success and link those objectives to levels of evaluation. As the figure illustrates, participant satisfaction objectives link to Level 1 evaluation; learning objectives link to Level 2 evaluation; application objectives link to Level 3 evaluation; impact objectives link to Level 4 evaluation; and ROI objectives link to the ROI outcome. If the application and impact objectives are not available, they have to be developed, using input from several groups such as job incumbents, program developers, facilitators, and on-the-job team leaders.

	Needs Assessment	Program Objectives	Evaluation
❺	Potential Payoff →	ROI →	ROI
❹	Business Needs →	Impact Objectives →	Business Impact
❸	Job Performance Needs →	Application Objectives →	Application
❷	Skill/Knowledge Needs →	Learning Objectives →	Learning
❶	Preferences →	Satisfaction Objectives →	Reaction

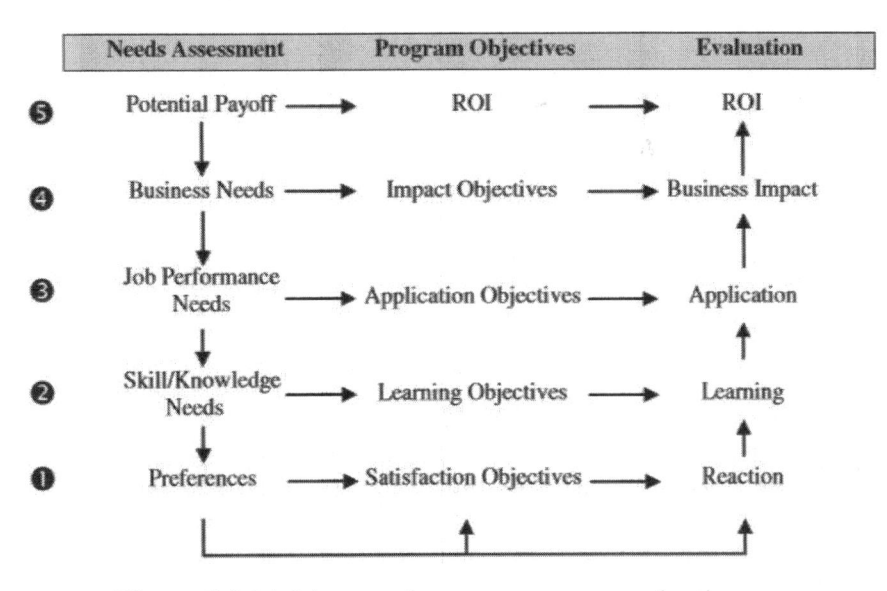

Figure 5.2 Linking needs assessment to evaluation

The data collection plan is an important part of the evaluation strategy and should be completed prior to moving forward with the training program. For existing training programs, the plan is completed before pursuing the ROI impact study. The plan provides a clear direction of what type of data will be collected, how it will be collected, who will provide the data, when it will be collected, and who will collect it.

Data collection is central to the ROI methodology. Both hard data (rep- resenting output, quality, cost, and time) and soft data (including job and customer satisfaction) are collected. Data are collected using a variety of methods including the following:

- Surveys are taken to determine the degrees to which participants are satisfied with the program, have learned skills and knowledge, and have used various aspects of the program. Survey responses are often developed on a sliding scale and usually represent perception data. Surveys are useful for Levels 1, 2, and 3 data.
- Questionnaires are usually more detailed than surveys and can be used to uncover a wide variety of data. Participants provide responses to a variety of open-ended and forced response questions. Questionnaires can be used to capture Levels 1, 2, 3, and 4 data.
- Tests are conducted to measure changes in knowledge and skills (Level 2). Tests come in a wide variety of formal (criterion-referenced tests, performance tests and simulations, and skill practices) and informal (facilitation assessment, self-assessment, and team assessment) methods.
- On-the-job observation captures actual skill application and use. Observations are particularly useful in customer service training and are more effective when the observer is either invisible or transparent. Observations are appropriate for Level 3 data.
- Interviews are conducted with participants to determine the extent to which learning has been used on the job. Interviews allow for probing to uncover specific

applications and are usually appropriate with Level 3 data, but can be used with Levels 1 and 2 data.
- Focus groups are conducted to determine the degree to which a group of participants has applied the training to job situations. Focus groups are usually appropriate with Level 3 data.
- Action plans and program assignments are developed by participants during the training program and are implemented on the job after the program is completed. Follow-ups provide evidence of training program success. Levels 3 and 4 data can be collected with action plans.
- Performance contracts are developed by the participant, the participant's supervisor, and the facilitator who all agree on job performance outcomes from training. Performance contracts are appropriate for both Levels 3 and 4 data.
- Business performance monitoring is useful where various performance records and operational data are examined for improvement. This method is particularly useful for Level 4 data.

The important challenge in data collection is to select the method or methods appropriate for the setting and the specific program, within the time and budget constraints of the organization.

An often overlooked issue in most evaluations is the process of isolating the effects of training. In this step of the process, specific strategies are explored that determine the amount of output performance directly related to the program. This step is essential because there are many factors that will influence performance data after training. The specific strategies of this step will pinpoint the amount of improvement directly related to the training program, resulting in increased accuracy and credibility of ROI calculations. The following techniques have been used by organizations to tackle this important issue:
- A control group arrangement is used to isolate training impact. With this strategy, one group receives training, while another similar group does not receive training. The

difference in the performance of the two groups is attributed to the training program. When properly set up and implemented, the control group arrangement is the most effective way to isolate the effects of training.
- Trend lines are used to project the values of specific output variables if training had not been undertaken. The projection is compared to the actual data after training, and the difference represents the estimate of the impact of training. Under certain conditions, this strategy can accurately isolate the training impact.
- When mathematical relationships between input and output variables are known, a forecasting model is used to isolate the effects of training. With this approach, the output variable is predicted using the forecasting model with the assumption that no training is conducted. The actual performance of the variable after the training is then compared with the forecasted value, which results in an estimate of the training impact.
- Participants estimate the amount of improvement related to training. With this approach, participants are provided with the total amount of improvement, on a preprogram and post program basis, and are asked to indicate the percent of the improvement that is actually related to the training program.
- Supervisors of participants estimate the impact of training on the output variables. With this approach, supervisors of participants are presented with the total amount of improvement and are asked to indicate the percent related to training.
- Senior management estimates the impact of training. In these cases, managers provide an estimate or "adjustment" to reflect the portion of the improvement related to the training program. While perhaps inaccurate, there are some advantages of having senior management involved in this process.
- Experts provide estimates of the impact of training on the performance variable. Because the estimates are based on

previous experience, the experts must be familiar with the type of training and the specific situation.
- When feasible, other influencing factors are identified and the impact estimated or calculated, leaving the remaining, unexplained improvement attributed to training. In this case, the influence of all of the other factors is developed, and training remains the one variable not accounted for in the analysis. The unexplained portion of the output is then attributed to training.
- In some situations, customers provide input on the extent to which training has influenced their decision to use a product or service. Although this strategy has limited applications, it can be quite useful in customer service and sales training.

Collectively, these techniques provide a comprehensive set of tools to tackle the important and critical issue of isolating the effects of training.

To calculate the return on investment, data collected in a Level 4 evaluation are converted to monetary values and compared to program costs. This requires a value to be placed on each unit of data connected with the program. A wide variety of techniques are available to convert data to monetary values. The specific techniques selected usually depends on the types of data and the situation:

- Output data are converted to profit contribution or cost savings. In this strategy, output increases are converted to monetary value based on their unit contribution to profit or the unit of cost reduction. Standard values for these items are readily available in most organizations.
- The cost of quality is calculated and quality improvements are directly converted to cost savings. Standard values for these items are available in many organizations.
- For programs where employee time is saved, the participants' wages and employee benefits are used to develop the value for time. Because a variety of programs focuses on improving the time required to complete projects, pro-

cesses, or daily activities, the value of time becomes an important and necessary issue. This is a standard formula in most organizations.
o Historical costs, developed from cost statements, are used when they are available for a specific variable. In this case, organizational cost data establishes the specific monetary cost savings of an improvement.
o When available, internal and external experts may be used to estimate a value for an improvement. In this situation, the credibility of the estimate hinges on the expertise and reputation of the individual.
o External databases are sometimes available to estimate the value or cost of data items. Research, government, and industry data- bases can provide important information for these values. The difficulty lies in finding a specific database related to the situation.
o Participants estimate the value of the data item. For this approach to be effective, participants must be capable of providing a value for the improvement.
o Supervisors and managers provide estimates when they are both willing and capable of assigning values to the improvement. This approach is especially useful when participants are not fully capable of providing this input or in situations where supervisors need to confirm or adjust the participant's estimate. This approach is particularly helpful to establish values for performance measures that are very important to senior management.
o Soft measures are linked mathematically to other measures that are easier to measure and value. This approach is particularly helpful when establishing values for measures that are very difficult to convert to monetary values, such as data often considered intangible, like customer satisfaction, employee satisfaction, grievances, and employee complaints.
o HRD staff estimates may be used to determine a value of an output data item. In these cases, it is essential for the estimates to be pro- vided on an unbiased basis.

The other part of the equation on a benefits/costs analysis is the program cost. Tabulating the costs involves monitoring or developing all of the related costs of the program targeted for the ROI calculation. Among the cost components that should be included are:

- the cost to design and develop the program, possibly prorated over the expected life of the program;
- the cost of all program materials provided to each participant;
- the cost for the instructor/facilitator, including preparation time as well as delivery time;
- the cost of the facilities for the training program;
- travel, lodging, and meal costs for the participants, if applicable;
- salaries plus employee benefits of the participants who attend the training; and
- administrative and overhead costs of the training function, allocated in some convenient way.

The return on investment is calculated using the program benefits and costs. The benefits/costs ratio (BCR) is the program benefits divided by cost. In formula form it is:

$$BCR = \frac{Program\ Benefits}{Program\ Costs}$$

Sometimes this ratio is stated as a cost/benefit ratio, although the formula is the same as BCR. The return on investment uses the net benefits divided by program costs. The net benefits are the program benefits minus the costs. In formula form, the ROI becomes:

$$ROI\ (\%) = \frac{Net\ Program\ Benefits}{Program\ Costs} \times 100$$

This is the same basic formula used in evaluating other investments where the ROI is traditionally reported as earnings divided by investment. The ROI from some training programs is high. For example, in sales, supervisory, and managerial training, the ROI can be quite high (frequently over 100%), while the ROI value for technical and operator training may be lower.

Finally keep in mind that the ROI methodology should not be applied to every program. It takes time and resources to create a valid and credible ROI study. it is appropriate now to underscore the types of programs where this technique is best suited. ROI is appropriate for those programs that:

- have a long life cycle. At some point in the life of the program, this level of accountability should be applied to the program.
- are very important to the organization in meeting its operating goals. These programs are designed to add value. ROI may be helpful to show that value.
- are closely linked to the organization's strategic initiatives. Any- thing this important needs a high level of accountability.
- are very expensive to implement. An expensive program, expending large amounts of company resources, should be subjected to this level of accountability.
- are highly visible and sometimes controversial. These programs often require this level of accountability to satisfy the critics.
- have a large target audience. If a program is designed for all employees, it may be a candidate for ROI.
- command the interest of a top executive group. If top executives are interested in knowing the impact, the ROI methodology should be applied.

These are only guidelines and should be considered in the context of the organization. Other criteria may also be appropriate. These criteria can be used in a scheme to sort out those programs most appropriate for this level of accountability.

Well we reached to the end of the book; I honestly do hope that you have found it useful and simple to understand.

Printed in Great Britain
by Amazon